Sir Charles Warren

The Temple or the Tomb.

Giving further evidence in favour of the authenticity of the present site of the Holy

Sepulchre

Sir Charles Warren

The Temple or the Tomb.
Giving further evidence in favour of the authenticity of the present site of the Holy Sepulchre

ISBN/EAN: 9783337816216

Printed in Europe, USA, Canada, Australia, Japan

Cover: Foto ©Lupo / pixelio.de

More available books at **www.hansebooks.com**

THE TEMPLE OR THE TOMB.

GIVING FURTHER EVIDENCE IN FAVOUR OF THE AUTHENTICITY OF THE
PRESENT SITE OF THE HOLY SEPULCHRE, AND POINTING OUT
SOME OF THE PRINCIPAL MISCONCEPTIONS CONTAINED
IN FERGUSSON'S 'HOLY SEPULCHRE' AND
'THE TEMPLES OF THE JEWS.'

BY

CHARLES WARREN,

FORMERLY IN CHARGE OF THE EXPLORATIONS AT JERUSALEM.

'It would be demanding a little too much from human nature to ask any one in his position to confess the errors of his ways, and to admit the success of a rival.'—*The Temples of the Jews*, p. vii.

LONDON:
RICHARD BENTLEY AND SON,
Publishers in Ordinary to Her Majesty the Queen.
1880.
[*All Rights Reserved.*]

CONTENTS.

	PAGE
PREFACE	iv

PART I.

THE PARALLEL HOLINESS OF ZION AND MORIAH	1
HISTORICAL ACCOUNT	2

PART II.

THE TOMB	29

PART III.

THE TEMPLE	76
THE TEMPLE OF HEROD	80

PART IV.

THE TEMPLE OR THE TOMB—INTRODUCTORY	107
SUBJECTS ON WHICH MR. FERGUSSON IS REFUTED	118

LIST OF ILLUSTRATIONS.

		PAGE
I.	CONTOURED PLAN OF JERUSALEM, 1876	33
II.	SKETCH OF JERUSALEM: TIME OF VESPASIAN	37
III.	THE TEMPLE OF HEROD	81
IV.	THE TEMPLE COURTS	95

PREFACE.

During the last fifteen years a vast amount of real information has been collected together concerning the sacred sites and existing buildings round about Jerusalem, which has in a great measure narrowed the old limits of controversy on topographical points, and left the various antagonists free to grapple more fully, and at leisure, with subjects of detail which a few years since could not be approached with any prospect of success, for want of knowledge of the general outlines.

On no theory have recent discoveries exercised so great an effect as on that original and bold hazard of Mr. Fergusson, the proposal that on the site of Solomon's Temple is the Sepulchre of our Lord; for to all who know anything of the subject, every additional item of information which recent years has afforded, has only more clearly demonstrated how entirely chimerical and illusory his views are, until at last the only sentiment remaining, is wonder why he should not abandon his theory in as cheerful a manner as practicable under the circumstances.

Apparently, however, this unhesitating writer has

no such intention, and with truly British characteristics, unable to realise that his cause is hopeless, that he has been signally vanquished by facts, he nails his colours to the mast, and crying 'No surrender!' pours out a broadside, even while in the act of sinking.

His last 'broadside' is entitled 'The Temples of the Jews,' a volume which continues to put forward with undiminished belief in his theory, and with considerable ingenuity, the views he has for so many years advocated; the ill effects of which I trust I may in some measure diminish or counteract by this volume, in which I intend to point out that many of his statements are incorrect, that his deductions cannot stand the ordeal of 'sound criticism,' and that local indications, historical facts, traditional reminiscences, architectural remains, and topographical details, all unite with one consent in protesting against the practicability of his theory.

Far be it from me to say that Mr. Fergusson has not assisted (after his manner) in promoting the discoveries which have so signally resulted in his own discomfiture, for it is obvious to all that the vehemence of his opinions, his warmth of expression, and strength of invective have stimulated his opponents to fresh exertions, to sift difficult questions, and to aid in the explorations, with an enthusiasm which could scarcely have been so strongly evinced had not party feeling strongly influenced them.

But now Mr. Fergusson's part is played out in this matter. The real battle rages in a different quarter, far away from his theory; the space is narrowed, and his last broadside may injure his individual antagonists, but cannot help his cause.

This being the case, there are many who, knowing that his theory is doomed, would rather it died a natural death. They do not, however, perceive that while in a moribund state it may do more harm than it ever did in full vigour, while attacked and kept under by the champions of facts; for his teaching is being industriously scattered over the land in atlases, in Biblical dictionaries, and in architectural text-books, and our youths are growing accustomed to the extraordinary errors he propounds before they are sufficiently experienced to judge for themselves. To use Mr. Fergusson's own words, 'Unless the heresy can be uprooted, it will inevitably come to be accepted in the course of time.'

There is, therefore, no time to be lost in pointing out the errors upon which he has grounded his theory, before they have spread too far and wide to be easily counteracted. This is more especially necessary, as Mr. Fergusson has stated constantly that his views have never yet been grappled with.

With this object before me, I propose to give a short historical account of the Holy Sepulchre, showing how all traditions, local indications, and other arguments, point out the present site of the Holy Sepulchre to be that which Constantine recovered, and on which he built—and further, that this was probably the true site of the Holy Sepulchre ; to give a short description of the ground about the Noble Sanctuary, showing how the Temple of Herod occupied the site where Mr. Fergusson would locate his hypothetical Holy Sepulchre ; and finally, I will analyse his works on the holy sites, pointing out a large number of very considerable errors which can be refuted. I will show that in the majority of cases his arguments are of no avail, and that his authority on such matters has not the weight he supposes ; that he cannot be considered to be a judge, for he does not sum up on both sides, but is simply a skilful advocate, depicting all his own arguments in brilliant colours, and endeavouring to throw discredit on his adversaries by various measures to which I will allude.

That he has constituted himself judge in his own cause will appear so strange to my readers that I will at once place them in possession of his own words on the subject ; that he is a very skilful advocate I will show further on. He says (p. 8, 'The Temples of the Jews') : 'In so far as my own personal experience goes, I have met no one during these thirty years able or willing to discuss the matter ; while if there is anyone in this country who has taken the trouble to master the subject in all its bearings, I can only express my regret that I am not acquainted with his name. Such controversies as have taken place in periodicals have generally hinged on some collateral points. No one, so far as I know, has, in print at least, grasped the really vital points at issue, and tried to argue either for or against them.' Page 6 : 'It may seem presumptuous, perhaps is so, on my part to venture to differ not only from those above-quoted, but from many others with whose views I do not agree ; but the fact, so far as I am able to judge, seems to be that no one, since the recently-acquired information became available, has taken the trouble and pains necessary to master the whole subject. No one, so far as I know, has gone through all the temples, from the Tabernacle to the destruction of the last by Titus, protracting each peculiarity as it arose, and superimposing each addition or alteration on the same plan. No one, while doing this, has attempted, in modern times, to co-ordinate the Bible, the historians, and the Talmud, so as to get a consistent answer out of their frequently discordant testimonies. Lightfoot and the Rabbis have attempted the latter task with great industry, but they failed for want of local knowledge and of the architectural skill necessary to solve the problem. Whether in this instance long study, combined with local knowledge and a certain amount of architectural skill, together with the new materials now available, will suffice to settle the question regarding the Temple, hitherto in dispute, remains to be seen. So far as I am capable of forming an opinion, the task now appears easy, and the result certain, within very narrow limits of deviation in any direction. . . . If, in short, Constantine did not build the Dome of the Rock, our architectural science is a delusion, unless some one else can bring forward new data from which new conclusions must be drawn.'

It will be seen from these statements that Mr. Fergusson presumes to judge what are the 'really vital points at issue,' and how they are to be argued, and who are fit to argue with him, and, in fact, that if they do not agree with him, 'architectural science is a delusion.'

I shall further show that he is incorrect in the principal arguments on which he founds his theory, and that he introduces grave errors which will be pointed out; and I have to submit that, if he is proved to be systematically wrong on the majority of points he brings forward, and which can be argued by the world generally, that the presumption is he is wrong on the remaining architectural argument, on which, apparently, he constitutes himself the sole authority.

But I will go further, and show that his architectural argument, by his own showing, hinges upon one point, and that upon this one point he is completely in error.

Still further will I go, and show by his own words, that even if his architectural argument was true for the west, he cannot show that it is true for the east.

He tells us: 'It may be broadly asserted that, in every instance of conflicting evidence, an appeal to style is at once allowed to override the most minute and circumstantial written testimony. . . . . In so far as Gothic architecture is concerned, this doctrine is now universally admitted as regards every country of Europe ; but many are not aware that the same is true of the classic styles, of the Saracenic, the Indian, and of every true style.'

And yet in the face of this he states of the Mosque at Hebron : ' We are therefore forced to adopt one of two hypotheses—either that the development of the style *was so much more rapid in the East than in the West*, as to admit of its being squeezed into the twenty years during which the bishopric of St. Abraham lasted (1167-87); or to assume that it was erected by a Christian architect for the Mahometans after the time of Saladin.'

We find Mr. Fergusson, therefore, himself pointing out that the styles in the East did not necessarily progress concurrently with those of the West, and that Christian architects may have worked for Moslem masters ; and yet we find him rigidly insisting that the style of a portion of the Dome of the Rock belongs to the age of Constantine, and no other. It seems to me that, by his own showing, the style may be that of Abd al Melek, wrought by Christian architects, more especially as he himself says that it is the only specimen of the kind in the world, and therefore there is nothing else to compare it with.

It is the more singular that he should insist on being the sole judge of this question in architecture, when we find arrayed against him the whole body of professional architects who have studied the matter, and whose opinions individually are at least as valuable as those of Mr. Fergusson, one of whom (Professor Willis) went so far as to say that his views were 'ludicrously impossible' ('The Temples of the Jews,' p. 196).

The peculiar manner in which Mr. Fergusson endeavours to detract from the value of the evidence or opinion of his opponents would be sufficiently amusing, were it not that he often oversteps the common limits of pleasantry and imputes motives which cannot be substantiated.

Of Professor Willis he says that, having once committed himself to a theory, it would be expecting too much to ask him to confess the error of his ways—'the late Professor Willis, of Cambridge, who was qualified, both by his knowledge of architecture and of the authorities, to give a decided opinion on the subject. He, however, had committed himself publicly to the authenticity of the Sepulchre in the town before my theory was published, and it would be demanding a little too much from human nature to ask anyone in his position to confess the error of his ways and to admit the success of a rival' ('The Temples of the Jews,' p. 7).

Of the late Mr. Lewin he disposes in a very summary manner: 'The late Mr. Lewin was another formidable opponent. He, however, knew nothing of architecture, and was familiar only with the classical branch of the literature of the subject; so that it is hardly to be wondered at that he missed the point of the argument.'

He can only dispose of the architectural knowledge of the Count de Vogüé by hinting that his religious opinions effectually biassed him: 'On the other hand, Count de Vogüé knows both the art and literature of the subject, and if it be not that his opinions are biassed by sincere devotion to his infallible Church, his reasoning on the subject is to me a mystery I cannot pretend to fathom.'

With Dr. Robinson he goes still further, and imputes to him a statement which he knew to be untrue: 'The great American, Dr. Edward Robinson, improves on this, and proves at once the absurdity of my views by inserting two definite articles into the text of Eusebius, and consequently making him say that the propylæa opened on *the* street of *the* Bazaar. *He knew, of course, that he was stating what was not true* when he put these words into the mouth of Eusebius; and it seems all the more strange that he should have condescended to this, as he had not even the excuse of religious zeal to justify the misrepresentation.'

The value of these imputations may be conjectured on comparing the separate translations: 'After these, the vestibule of the whole group of buildings, situated in *the middle of a broad agora*' ('The Temples of the Jews,' p. 238). 'Beyond this, in the very *midst of the street of the market*,' etc. (Robinson, 'Bib. Researches,' 8). 'After these, in the midst of *the open market-place*' (Euseb., 'Life of Constantine,' iii. ch. xxxiii).

Is this discrepancy sufficient for Dr. Robinson to

b

be charged with wilful misrepresentation and stating what he knew was not true? If so, what is to be said of Mr. Fergusson regarding his very numerous errors and inaccuracies, which I shall point out?

In a recent discussion on Buddhist architecture, Colonel Yule, in alluding to a theory of Mr. Fergusson's, states: 'Most things he says are striking and suggestive, and one at least hesitates to oppose them;' and this appears to be a most happy description of his theories. They are striking and suggestive there can be no doubt, but they are not correct. Most persons hesitate to oppose his theories because of the warmth of expression and strength of invective in which he indulges. And he is not even content with this treatment of living or recent authorities; he must also find fault with early writers who do not concur in his views, and especially with William of Tyre, whose evidence is strongly against him. Moreover he does not stop at finding fault with profane writings, but acknowledges that in order to support his argument he has to do 'considerable violence to the text' of the Book of Exodus; he tries to prove that the text of the Book of Ezekiel is wrong; he accuses the Book of Chronicles of exaggeration, and proposes that the Israelites derived the shape of the Tabernacle from some wandering tribe of Midianites. These matters I shall call attention to as I proceed.

In writing this volume I have not necessarily reiterated the former arguments by which authors have previously defeated Mr. Fergusson; they are to be found in the works of Robinson, Williams, Lewin, Palmer and Besant, and others : for without them I think I have given sufficient proof that his theories are not to be relied on, that his statements are in many cases very inaccurate, and that notwithstanding his assertions to the contrary, the Temple of Herod did occupy the ground on which he would place the Holy Sepulchre, and that the Holy Sepulchre did occupy the present site.

THE TEMPLE OR THE TOMB.

PART I.

THE PARALLEL HOLINESS OF ZION AND MORIAH.

'The stone of Israel.'

THE chief information extant on the subject of the positions of Jerusalem and Zion, is to be found in the historical and poetical books of the Old Testament, the Books of the Maccabees, the Works of Josephus, and the Talmud.

Of these five sources of information, the two first are portions of the inspired writings, and therefore to them must we look for our most trustworthy information; in doing so, however, we must take into due consideration the licence of expression permitted in poetical works, and on this account it is proposed to examine the subject primarily from the historical books: and, with this in view, I have extracted and placed somewhat in the form of a continuous narrative all the information that can be found bearing on the subject.

From these extracts it will appear that Jerusalem, Zion, and Moriah were not interchangeable terms, but were fixed places—the former being the Holy City as a whole, the two latter being definite and distinct portions of the Holy City, whose positions can exactly be determined, knowing as we do one of them (Moriah) at the present day.

Passing to the poetical books, we shall find that a parallelism exists with regard to the holiness of Mounts Zion and Moriah, which explains the apparent discrepancies hitherto creating so many difficulties in fixing their sites, but at the same time we can obtain no clue from these books alone as to the absolute or relative meanings of the terms Jerusalem and Zion.

Hence passing to the Books of the Maccabees, we shall find that this parallelism accounts for their change in the position of Sion; and following up this clue, we shall find that the accounts of Josephus are connected with those of the Old Testament, and through his account we shall bring down the record of the position of Zion, until we can fix it with considerable precision at the present day.

These results differ in a great degree from the results of those who have previously written upon the subject, and in whose proposals great difficulties have always been experienced. These difficulties, I believe, are now removed by the discovery I have made of the parallel holiness of Mounts Zion and Moriah, which I will now proceed to point out.

Historical Account.

Joshua x. 1.—Adoni-zedec, king of Jerusalem [slain by Joshua].

Judges i. 7-8.—And they brought him to Jerusalem, and there he died . . . Now the children of Judah had fought against Jerusalem, and had taken it, and smitten it with the edge of the sword, and set the city on fire.

Joshua xv. 63.—As for the Jebusites, the inhabitants of Jerusalem, the children of Judah could not drive them out; but the Jebusites dwell with the children of Judah at Jerusalem unto this day.

Joshua xviii. 21.—Now the cities of the tribe of the children of Benjamin according to their families were . . . Jerusalem.

Judges i. 21.—And the children of Benjamin did not drive out the Jebusites that inhabited Jerusalem; but the Jebusites dwell with the children of Benjamin in Jerusalem unto this day.

Judges xix. 1, 10-12.—A certain Levite . . . came over against Jebus, which is Jerusalem; . . . and the servant said, Come, I pray thee, and let us turn into the city of the Jebusites, and lodge in it. And his master said, We will not turn aside hither into the city of a stranger, that is not of the children of Israel.

1 *Samuel* xvii. 54.—And David took the head of the Philistine, and brought it to Jerusalem.

2 *Samuel* v. 6-9.—And the king and his men went to Jerusalem unto the Jebusites, the inhabitants of the land . . . Nevertheless David took the stronghold of Zion; the same is the city of David. And David said on that day, Whosoever getteth up to the gutter, and smiteth the Jebusites . . . So David dwelt in the fort, and called it the city of David. And David built round about from Millo and inward.

1 *Chron.* xi. 4.—And David and all Israel went to Jerusalem, which is Jebus; where the Jebusites were the inhabitants of the land. And the inhabitants of

Jebus said to David, Thou shalt not come hither. Nevertheless, David took the castle of Zion, which is the city of David. And David dwelt in the castle; therefore they called it the city of David. And he built the city round about, even from Millo round about; and Joab repaired the rest of the city.

1 *Chron.* xiv. 3.—And David took more wives at Jerusalem.

1 *Chron.* xv. 1.—And David made him houses in the city of David, and prepared a place for the ark of God, and pitched for it a tent.

2 *Samuel* vi. 12.—So David went and brought up the ark of God from the house of Obed-edom into the city of David with gladness . . . And as the ark of the Lord came into the city of David, Michal, Saul's daughter, looked through a window, and saw David leaping and dancing before the Lord . . . And they brought in the ark of the Lord, and set it in his place, in the midst of the tabernacle that David had pitched for it: and David offered burnt-offerings and peace-offerings before the Lord.

1 *Chron.* xvi. 37.—So he left there before the ark of the covenant of the Lord Asaph and his brethren, to minister before the ark continually, as every day's work required. And Obed-edom and their brethren, threescore and eight . . . And Zadok the priest, and his brethren the priests, before the tabernacle of the Lord in the high place that was at Gibeon.

1 *Chron.* xvii. 1.—Now it came to pass, as David sat in his house, that David said to Nathan the prophet, Lo, I dwell in an house of cedars, but the ark of the covenant of the Lord remaineth under curtains.

2 *Samuel* xi. 1.—But David tarried still at Jerusalem.

2 *Samuel* xv. 17.—And the king went forth . . . and lo, Zadok also, and all the Levites were with him, bearing the ark of the covenant of God. And the king said unto Zadok, Carry back the ark of God into the city. Zadok therefore and Abiathar carried the ark of God again to Jerusalem.

2 *Samuel* xx. 3.—And David came to his house at Jerusalem.

1 *Chron.* xxi. 15.—And God sent an angel unto Jerusalem to destroy it . . . And the angel of the Lord stood by the threshing-floor of Ornan the Jebusite. And David lifted up his eyes, and saw the angel of the Lord stand between earth and heaven, having a drawn sword in his hand stretched out over Jerusalem. . . . Then the angel of the Lord commanded Gad to say to David, that David should go up, and set up an altar unto the Lord in the threshing-floor of Ornan the Jebusite. And David went up at the saying of Gad . . . And Ornan turned back and saw the angel; and his four sons with him hid themselves. Now Ornan was threshing wheat. And as David came to Ornan, Ornan looked and saw David, and went out of the threshing-floor, and bowed himself to David with his face to the ground. Then David said to Ornan, Grant me the place of this threshing-floor, that I may build an altar therein unto the Lord. . . . And David built there an altar unto the Lord, and offered burnt-offerings and peace-offerings, and called upon the Lord; and He answered him from heaven by fire, upon the altar of burnt-offering . . . at that time when David saw that the Lord had answered him in the threshing-floor of Ornan the Jebusite, then he sacrificed there. For the tabernacle of the Lord, which Moses made in the wilderness, and the altar of

the burnt-offering, were at that season in the high-place at Gibeon.

2 *Chron.* xxii. 1.—Then David said, This is the house of the Lord God, and this is the altar of the burnt offering of Israel.

1 *Kings* ii. 10.—So David slept with his fathers, and was buried in the city of David.

1 *Kings* iii. 1.—And Solomon took Pharaoh's daughter, and brought her into the city of David, until he had made an end of building his own house, and the house of the Lord, and the wall of Jerusalem round about . . . And the king went to Gibeon to sacrifice there.

2 *Chron.* iii. 1.—Then Solomon began to build the house of the Lord at Jerusalem in Mount Moriah, when the Lord appeared unto David his father, in the place that David had prepared in the threshing-floor of Ornan the Jebusite.

1 *Kings* viii. 1.—Then Solomon assembled the elders of Israel and all the heads of the tribes, the chief of the fathers of the children of Israel, unto King Solomon in Jerusalem, that they might bring up the ark of the covenant of the Lord out of the city of David, which is Zion.

2 *Chron.* viii. 11.—And Solomon brought up the daughter of Pharaoh out of the city of David unto the house that he had built for her : for he said, My wife shall not dwell in the house of David, king of Israel, because the places are holy, whereunto the ark of the Lord hath come.

2 *Chron.* ix. 3.—And when the queen of Sheba had seen the wisdom of Solomon, and the house that he had built . . . and his ascent by which he went up into the house of the Lord, there was no more spirit in her.

1 *Kings* xi. 27.— . . . Solomon built Millo, and

repaired the breaches of the city of David his father
. . . And Solomon slept with his fathers, and was
buried in the city of David his father.

2 *Chron.* xx. 28.—And they came to Jerusalem
with psalteries and trumpets into the house of the
Lord.

2 *Chron.* xxi. 20.— . . . Howbeit they buried him
[Jehoram] in the city of David, but not in the
sepulchres of the kings.

2 *Kings* xii. 20.— . . . and slew Joash in the house
of Millo that goeth down to Silla.

2 *Kings* xiv. 13.—And Jehoash, king of Israel . . .
broke down the wall of Jerusalem from the gate of
Ephraim unto the corner gate, four hundred cubits.

2 *Chron.* xxviii. 27.—And Ahaz slept with his
fathers, and they buried him in the city, even in
Jerusalem ; but they brought him not into the
sepulchres of the kings of Israel.

2 *Chron.* xxx. 1.— . . . house of the Lord at
Jerusalem.

2 *Chron.* xxxii. 5.— . . . and repaired Millo in the
city of David.

2 *Kings* xviii. 22 ; 2 *Chron.* xxxiii. 30 ; 2 *Chron.*
xxiii. 4.

2 *Chron.* xxiii. 7.—In this house, and in Jerusalem.

2 *Kings* xix. 21.—The virgin the daughter of Zion
hath despised thee, and laughed thee to scorn ; the
daughter of Jerusalem hath shaken her head at thee.—
31. For out of Jerusalem shall go forth a remnant,
and they that escape out of Mount Zion.

2 *Kings* xxi. 4.

2 *Chron.* xxxiv. 29.—Then the king sent and
gathered together all the elders of Judah and Jerusalem . . .—32. And he caused all that were present
in Jerusalem and Benjamin to stand to it.

2 *Chron.* xxxvi. 14.— . . . and polluted the house of the Lord which he had hallowed in Jerusalem.— 19. And they burnt the house of God, and brake down the wall of Jerusalem, and burnt all the palaces thereof with fire, and destroyed all the goodly vessels thereof.

Ezra speaks of the house of the Lord in and at Jerusalem.

From the above passages we find that, in the time of Joshua, Jerusalem was a city with a king, Adonizedec. On the partition of Palestine among the tribes of Israel, we find Jerusalem allotted to Benjamin, the boundary-line running south of Jebus; and the children of Benjamin could not drive the Jebusites out, but dwelt with them. And again, though Jerusalem is not allotted to Judah, we find Judah taking and burning Jerusalem, and putting the inhabitants to the sword; and, further on, that Judah could not drive the Jebusites out, but dwelt with them. Now from this alone we must conclude that some part of Jerusalem lay in the tribe of Judah, although the boundary-line passing south of Jerusalem places it in Benjamin. But still there would exist a confusion in the mind upon the subject were we not able, from the succeeding history, to conclude that there were two portions to Jerusalem in the earliest times—a citadel and a suburb: a portion so well fortified that the children of Benjamin could not take it, and a part badly fortified, which Benjamin and Judah did take and dwell in. It is, however, better to let this question wait until we arrive at a correct notion of the appearance of Jerusalem when taken by King David. We find, then, that David went to Jerusalem, which is Jebus, and took the stronghold or castle of Zion, which, in consequence, received the name of the city of David :

' And he dwelt in Zion, which is the city of David, and he built the city round about, even from Millo round about, and Joab repaired the remainder of the city.'

Now it is evident that this ' city,' Zion, was not a mere tower, for we hear afterwards of David's house being built there ; and the household for his families was there ; and the *houses* for the ark of God, in which we may presume were offices for Asaph and his brethren, and Obed-edom with their brethren, threescore and eight, and the priests ; and the Royal Sepulchres were also there, and Millo,* which latter, from the allusions to it, may be supposed to have been the *dernier-ressort*, the strongest point in Zion. It is thus evident that Zion fully deserved the name of the ' city ' of David, and that it was a stronghold of very considerable extent ; but, on the other hand, it is no less certain that it formed part and was the fortress of Jerusalem. There are many passages to prove this in the historical books, and not one to show that Jerusalem was a part of Zion. David took more

* Millo is rendered in the Septuagint by ἡ ἄκρα (the citadel) a word used by Josephus and Books of Maccabees for the north western hill where I locate Zion or the City of David.

wives at Jerusalem, and children were born to him in Jerusalem. When Joab went against Ammon David tarried at Jerusalem; when David fled from Jerusalem, the priests carried the ark of God *again* to Jerusalem, and they tarried there; and David came to his house at Jerusalem. Now, if Zion were not a part of Jerusalem, it could not be said that the ark was brought *again* to Jerusalem, after it had been deposited in Zion; and the same with David's house. Now, it is equally clear that Zion was not synonymous or co-extensive with Jerusalem, for we find Zion is only mentioned when it is desirable to fix the particular position of some building, etc., while Jerusalem is used to denote the city generally. Thus, having once said that David's house was in Zion, it was not necessary to keep recurring to that fact; but the term Jerusalem is used generally, except in a few instances, where it is necessary to make a distinction between the several parts of Jerusalem; for example, David's burial, the bringing of Pharaoh's daughter to the city of David until another house should be built for her in Jerusalem, the taking of the ark out of Zion to the temple, etc. We have not a single instance in the historical books of the term Zion, or the city of David, being used for the whole city.

It appears, then, that Jerusalem was the name for the whole city, walled and unwalled, and that Zion, the city of David, was the name for a portion of it better fortified than the rest: this appears also when David built the city round about, and Joab repaired the remainder of the city, and when Solomon built the walls of Jerusalem, and repaired the breaches of the city of David his father. It is also obvious that Zion was on the northern side of the Holy City, for it is said to have been within the boundary of Benjamin, while the suburbs of Jerusalem were in Judah.

We may now proceed to examine the question as to Mount Moriah.

This hill seems in David's time to have been close to and without the city of Jerusalem. It would hardly be necessary to point out that Mounts Zion and Moriah were distinct hills, were it not that of late years they have been pronounced by some writers to be identical. In the first place, for many years after King David captured Jerusalem, Zion was a royal city, while Moriah must have been beyond Jerusalem, and was the private property of a sheikh or chieftain of the Jebusites. Then, again, David had to go up to Mount Moriah, which he could not have done had the two been identical; then we have the grand ceremony of bringing the ark of. God *out of the city of David, which is Zion,* up to Mount Moriah.

Two of the great acts of Solomon's life were, building the house of the Lord on Mount Moriah, and building the walls of Jerusalem, and thus joining Moriah to and making it part of the Holy City; and we have every reason to suppose that Moriah was distinct from Zion; for while Zion, the city of David, is frequently mentioned with reference to the royal sepulchres, etc., we have, after the building of the

Temple, Jerusalem marked as the holy place *par excellence*. For example, when David goes up at first to the threshing-floor, he says, 'This is the house of the Lord God.' Again, we have, 'But I have chosen Jerusalem that my name may be there . . . Jerusalem the city which I have chosen to put my name there . . . And they came to Jerusalem . . . unto the house of the Lord . . . House of the Lord at Jerusalem . . . In Jerusalem shall my name be for ever . . . In Jerusalem will I put my name . . . the house of the Lord which he had hallowed in Jerusalem ;'— and in no single instance in the historical books is this said of Zion after the building of the Temple. To make this the more remarkable, we have two instances where the historian, quoting from the poetical book of Isaiah, says, 'The virgin the daughter of Zion hath despised thee ; the daughter of Jerusalem hath shaken her head at thee.'—'For out of Jerusalem shall go forth a remnant, and they that escape out of Mount Zion.' Thus marking the difference in mentioning the Holy City in prose and poetry. We have, then, the Holy City of Jerusalem containing at least two distinct hills, which are Zion and Moriah, the remaining portion of the city probably resting on a third hill and the intermediate valleys. Now, if we place three round-shot close together, we have a rough model of Jerusalem in the time of Solomon, the shot to the north-west being Mount Zion, that to the east Moriah, and that to the south-west the remainder of Jerusalem.

Thus, having the figure of Jerusalem in our minds,

we may again recur to the question of the boundary-line between the two tribes, merely to notice 2 Chron. xxxiv. 29, where it says—' the elders of Judah and Jerusalem—all that were present in Jerusalem and Benjamin'—which successively places Jerusalem within the boundary of each tribe. And as there can be little doubt that Zion the stronghold was in Benjamin, we have nearly the certainty that the remainder of the Holy City was to the south of Zion in Judah.

And now we come to mention what appears to be the key to the topography of the Holy City, the parallel holiness of Mounts Zion and Moriah.

During the latter years of King David's life Moriah was selected as the abode of God's name, but Mount Zion was the hill on which the ark of God was placed during the full tide of David's strength and successes, and on which it rested throughout his trying family troubles ; and there can be little doubt that a large number of his Psalms were penned during that period. No wonder then that he should continually sing the praises of Zion ; the stronghold which he had captured after it had resisted the arms of Israel nigh four hundred years—the house of the Lord where he offered up burnt-offerings and peace-offerings—the site of his palace—where his children were born—where he brought up Absalom—the royal city in which he had built so much and where he probably had arranged for his burial ; no wonder then that this city of David was made famous in his songs. And further, Zion was a holy hill not only during part of David's reign ;

even after he had said of Mount Moriah, 'This is the house of the Lord God,' Zion still remained a holy place, the seat of the ark of God ; and in it Solomon, when anointed king, offered burnt and peace-offerings ; and even after the ark of God had been taken out of the city of David and placed on Mount Moriah, Zion still appears to have remained holy ; for did not King Solomon take his wife, the daughter of Pharaoh, out of the city of David unto a house he had built for her? for he said, ' My wife shall not dwell in the house of David, king of Israel, for the places are holy whereunto the ark of the Lord hath come.' This, then, is apparently the key to the great question about Mounts Zion and Moriah.

Mount Moriah was added to Jerusalem, and therefore we have, in the historical books, the mention of the 'Lord's name in Jerusalem ;' but in the poetical books the first songs were penned before ever David knew of the existence of Mount Moriah beyond its being the threshing-floor of a Jebusite ; and all his thoughts were concentrated on Zion, the seat of the ark of God. Therefore it is we have in those Psalms ascribed to David such expressions as ' My holy hill of Zion ; . . . Lord which dwelleth in Zion.' But it is important to remark, that in Psalm lxviii., ascribed to David at the dedication of the materials for the future Temple on Mount Moriah, he at once marks the difference, and for the first time says, ' Because of thy temple at Jerusalem.' In Psalm cxxii. we also find Jerusalem alone spoken of as the house of God. We therefore come to the conclusion that until the dedication of the materials for the Temple on Mount Moriah, King David celebrated the praises of Zion alone, but that afterwards he indifferently used the names either of Jerusalem or Zion, or used them both in apposition, taking advantage of that beautiful parallelism for which Hebrew poetry is noted, and which, though it runs throughout the earlier Psalms, is not applied to Jerusalem itself until about the forty-seventh to the fifty-first Psalm, when Jerusalem possessed two holy places in one.

If we now examine the poetical books, we shall find Zion, or Mount Zion, used indifferently and vaguely, first, for the city of Jerusalem generally; secondly, for the city of David, Zion proper; thirdly, for the house of God in a figurative sense. We also find Jerusalem used in the first and third senses, if not in the second; but by far the greater number of passages mention Jerusalem or Zion in a figurative sense—meaning the children of Judah generally, or the abode of God's name—and not in such a manner as to denote any particular piece of ground.

A few examples are here given:

1. *Zion, meaning the whole City of Jerusalem.*

Psalm cxlix. 2.—Let the children of Zion be joyful in their king.

Psalm lxxxvii. 2.—Her foundation is upon the holy hills: the Lord loveth the gates of Zion more than all the dwellings of Jacob.

Isaiah xxxii. 14.—The sinners in Zion are afraid.

Joel ii. 1.—Blow ye the trumpet in Zion, and sound an alarm in my holy mountain.

2. *Zion, meaning Zion proper, the City of David.*

Ps. xlviii. 12.—Beautiful for situation,
The joy of the whole earth,
The mountain of Zion,
The sides of the north,
The city of the great King.

* * * *

Walk about Zion, and go round
about her,
Tell the towers thereof.
Mark ye well her bulwarks,
Consider her palaces.

Isaiah xxx. 19.—For the people shall dwell in Zion at Jerusalem.

Micah iv. 7, 8.—And the Lord shall reign over them in mount Zion from henceforth even for ever. And thou, O town of the flock, the stronghold of the daughter of Zion, unto thee shall it come, even the first dominion.

3. *Zion, meaning the House of God.*

Psalm ix. 11.—Sing praises to the Lord which dwelleth in Zion.

Psalm xcix. 2.—The Lord is great in Zion.

Psalm cxxxii. 13.—For the Lord hath chosen Zion; He hath desired it for His habitation.

Isaiah viii. 18.—The Lord of hosts, which dwelleth in Zion.

Jeremiah viii. 19.—Is not the Lord in Zion?

Micah iv. 7.—And the Lord shall reign over them in mount Zion from henceforth, even for ever.

With regard to *Jerusalem*, we of course find the term used frequently in its proper sense, as

Psalms lxxiv. 1 ; cxx. 2 ; *Ezekiel* iv. 7.

But we also find—

Jerusalem, meaning the House of God.

Psalm lxviii. 29.—Because of Thy temple at Jerusalem.
Psalm cxxii. 1, 2.—Let us go into the house of the Lord. Our feet shall stand within thy gates, O Jerusalem.
Psalm cxxxvii. 5.—If I forget thee, O Jerusalem.
Isaiah xxvii. 13.—And shall worship the Lord in the holy mount at Jerusalem.
Isaiah lxii. 17.— . . . till He make Jerusalem a praise in the earth.
Jeremiah iii. 7.— . . . to the name of the Lord, to Jerusalem.
Zechariah ii. 12.—And shall choose Jerusalem again.

We thus find that after the latter days of King David, Jerusalem or Zion, when mentioned separately in the poetical books, are used as interchangeable terms, meaning either the Holy City or the House of God. We also find this to be the case in the parallel passages ; so much so, that Judah or Israel also stand in places for the sanctuary.

Ps. lxxvi. 1, 2.—In Judah is God known,
His name is great in Israel.
In Salem also is His tabernacle,
And His dwelling-place in Zion.

Psalm cxiv. 2.—Judah was His sanctuary,
   And Israel His dominion.
Ps. cxxxv. 21.—Blessed be the Lord out of Zion,
   Which dwelleth at Jerusalem.
Is. ii. 3.—For out of Zion shall go forth the law,
   And the word of the Lord from Jerusalem.
Joel iii. 16.—The Lord also shall roar out of Zion,
   And utter His voice from Jerusalem.
Zech. viii. 3.—I am returned unto Zion,
   And will dwell in the midst of Jerusalem.

Again, if we proceed further, we shall find that Jerusalem and Zion are denounced both singly and in the parallel passages.

Isaiah iii. 17.—Therefore the Lord will smite with a scab the crown of the head of the daughters of Zion, and the Lord will discover their secret parts.
Isaiah iv. 4.—When the Lord shall have washed away the filth of the daughters of Zion, and shall have purged the blood of Jerusalem . . .
Isaiah xxxiii. 14.—The sinners in Zion are afraid.
Jeremiah xiv. 19.—Hath thy soul lothed Zion?
Jeremiah xxx. 17.—This is Zion whom no man seeketh after.
Micah iii. 10.—They build up Zion with blood,
   And Jerusalem with iniquity.

It thus appears from the preceding examples that from the poetical books alone, no idea of the relative or absolute meanings of Jerusalem and Zion can be obtained; it yet, however, remains to be shown that from the parallel passages, when taken individually, it can be proved that Jerusalem and Zion *are the same*, and that they *are different* places. For this purpose we will quote the following Psalms:

Psalm xcviii. 8; civ. 18; cxiv. 2; cxxxii. 4; cxxii. 7; vi. 5; cxlvii. 12.

Now we have in these several instances of constructive parallelism, in which there is equality between the different propositions, though they differ considerably in degree in each extract. Thus, take Psalm xcviii. 8, and compare it with cxxxii. 4, or vi. 5. Again, if we take a number of them like Psalm xcviii. 8, we may prove Jerusalem to be different from Zion in Psalm cxxvii. 12; and if we take several, like Psalm cxxxvii. 4, or vi. 5, we may prove Jerusalem to be Zion in that same verse of Psalm cxlvii. It is thus evident that the parallel passages also, except in special cases, are worthless so far as settling the topography of Jerusalem is concerned; and that the topography of the poetical books can only be read by the light of the historical books. It is very important to establish that the poetical books are unable of themselves to settle the disputed points, because hitherto much stress has been placed on the prominence given to Zion in them. It is to be observed that the passages bearing directly on the subject which were extracted from the poetical books, and of which twenty-six refer to Jerusalem, fifty-eight to Zion, and sixty-two to Jerusalem, Zion, Judah, etc., are all in parallelism.

It now remains to point out Psalm xlviii. as being perhaps an exception to the general rule, for in this Zion appears from its palaces, etc., to mean the stronghold of David, and if so we have direct proof that it stood on the northern side of the city. Another has a peculiar reference. Isaiah xxxi. 4 : 'To fight for Mount Zion and the hill thereof.'

We thus appear to have shown how, in the poetical works, up to the dedication of the materials for the Temple the praises of Zion alone were sung, and that after that time advantage was taken of the Hebrew style to parallel the present holiness of Moriah with the past glories of Zion : thus giving to the poems a strength and beauty which they lacked before.

It is to be observed that in general a preference is given to Zion, the elder city in holiness, except in the Book of the Prophet Zechariah, where Jerusalem appears to be preferred ; and it is natural to suppose that Zion should in song have the preference, since not only do the prophets copy their style each from the other, thus originally deriving it from David, but Zion had of itself a more unmixed, even if an inferior, holiness to Jerusalem, for it had contained only the ark of God and the royal palaces, etc., while Jerusalem, besides containing the holy places (Zion and Moriah), was the abode of the Jebusites and other original Gentile inhabitants of the land. It is evident, then, how Zion might gradually acquire in the minds of the people a meaning synonymous with the Temple, except to those who were well acquainted with the historical books.

Having now obtained the leading features of the topography of Jerusalem from the historical books, and having seen that the poetical books can only be read by the aid of the former, we pass on to the Books of the Maccabees. We have already anticipated that the constant use of the Psalms of David would connect the name of Zion with the house of the Lord. This we find to be the case in the Books of the Maccabees, written more than 300 years after the time of the prophet Nehemiah, during which interval Jerusalem was repeatedly besieged and desolated. At this time, then, we find the city of David occupied by a foreign garrison, and still the stronghold of the city, from whence the foreign soldiers descended to molest the Jews going up to the sanctuary (now called Sion). Here we see the effects of poetry. The historical books may be out of mind, the prophets may be forgotten ; but the songs of David descend from father to sons by word of mouth, and still reign in the hearts of all. Hence they call the sanctuary (though changed in position) Mount Sion.

Extracts from the Books of the Maccabees.—1 Macc. i. 33. Then builded they the city of David with a great and strong wall, and with mighty towers and made a stronghold (an Akra) for them.

iv. 37.— ... And went up into Mount Sion. And when they saw the sanctuary desolate and the altar profaned ...

v. 54.—So they went up to Mount Sion with joy and gladness, where they offered burnt-offerings ...

Now crossing over to Josephus, we find the same tale of the Maccabees told in different language; but mention is not made of the Zion of David or the Sion of the Maccabees. How could he mention them by name? As an historian he must have been aware of the identity between the city of David and Zion (his Akra on north-western hill of Jerusalem), but he could not call it Zion; to do so would have caused a confusion in his story to anybody who had also access to the Books of the Maccabees; he therefore wisely left the name out altogether. Therefore, as Josephus describes the topography of Jerusalem in the time of Herod, and gives the position of Zion (the city of David of the Maccabees), his Macedonian Akra, we have a connecting link throughout.

The point marked on the Ordnance Survey plan as Akra, the present Sarai, the palace of Helena, at Takiyeh, (on the north-western hill) appears to be the site where Zion once was, and is not; for the Hasmoneans, working night and day for three years, cut away the old stronghold of David, and by that act destroyed the parallelism between the holy places, leaving Moriah* alone to represent the abode of God's name.

When Jerusalem came under the Roman and Christian rule, and the songs of David held diminished sway, history began to be examined, and it is likely that the term Zion should again designate the

* The name *Moriah* is mentioned but once in the historical books, but it is then distinctly stated to be the name of the mount on which the Temple was built.

city of David; but the hill had disappeared, and therefore it is probable that the adjoining hill, other than the Temple, should be called Zion; and this we find to be the case.

We have found, then, in the historical books of the Old Testament, Jerusalem containing the city of David or Zion,* Mount Moriah or the Temple, and the remainder of the city. Again, in 1 Maccabees, we find Jerusalem containing the same city of David—called the tower or fortress (ἡ ἄκρα)—the same Temple, and the remainder of the city. And in Josephus we find Jerusalem containing the same Temple, a lower city (ἡ ἄκρα) and an upper city; but the names Zion, Sion, and Moriah are not mentioned; the city of David is mentioned, and it will be shown that it was used to designate the lower city of King David's time, to which was joined the Akra, the citadel, and that after this circumstance the whole of the lower city, including the citadel, was called Akra. Now of the two cities, the upper and the lower, it is evident, without any doubt, that the latter, the lower city, the Akra of Josephus, corresponds to, and is identical with, the city of David, or fortress or Akra of the Maccabees, and therefore with the city of David or Zion of the historical books; but we know where the upper city was, for the upper city exists at the present day, viz., the hill lying south of the road leading from the Jaffa Gate to the Bab es-Silsile, and including the Armenian and Jewish quarters, and

* Containing the Millo or Akra of the Septuagint.

probably also part of the hill to the south, outside the walls. We have positive proof of this being the upper city of Josephus, from his statement that the palace of Agrippa overlooked the Temple, that it was in the upper city, and connected with the Xystus, and from thence by a bridge with the Temple; and in Jerusalem no other site can be found for this palace but on the high ground overlooking the Haram area. Now, having fixed the site of the upper city, the lower city, Akra, falls into its place to the north, about et-Takiyeh, or the palace of Helena (where is the word Akra on the Ordnance Survey plan); for Akra could not have been south of the upper city as here fixed, and if further to the north than et-Takiyeh, it would have been on the other side of the valley, and in such a position that the Macedonian garrison, quartered in it, could not have disturbed the Jews who went up to the Temple, as described in 1 Maccabees.

Now, though Josephus does not actually mention Zion, we ought, if he be an accurate writer, to be able to infer from his language where he supposes Zion to have been. In proving this and looking into the matter we find a striking peculiarity in his topography, viz., his vagueness in speaking of the topography of the past, his precision in detailing the walls and buildings which existed about his own time; this is greatly in contrast with the precision throughout the historical books and 1 Maccabees, and causes the topographical account of Josephus up to the time of the death of

Simon Maccabeus to be of secondary consideration. Thus we find Josephus frequently adding to and amplifying the Biblical stories; but yet it does not appear in any case that he gives any help in the topography; on the contrary, he always mentions Jerusalem in such general terms as to lead one to suppose that he was himself uncertain of the identity of its various portions, as he knew it, with those which are mentioned in the Biblical account. It is, however, clear that he is in accord with the historical books and 1 Maccabees in making Zion, the city of David, coincide with Akra, the lower city:

Antiquities, vii. 3 :—' So he took the lower city by force, but the citadel (ἄκρα) held out still. When David had cast the Jebusites out of the citadel (ἄκρα) he also rebuilt Jerusalem, and named it the city of David. Now when he had chosen Jerusalem to be his royal city . . . a royal palace at Jerusalem. Now David made buildings round about the lower city; he also *joined the citadel* (ἄκρα) *to it and made it one body;* and when he had encompassed all with walls he appointed Joab to take care of them.'

Bel., v. 4, § 1 :—' Of these hills, that which contains the upper city is much higher . . . But the other hill, which is called " Akra," and *sustains the lower city. . .*'

We have, then, David taking the lower city and afterwards Akra (or in the Biblical account Zion), and then joining all in one, so that the whole lower city with its citadel took the name of Akra. Josephus gives, however (*B. J.*, v. 4, § 1), another account, which says that David called the upper city the fortress (φρούριον); and some writers have identified the upper city, which David called the fortress, with the Akra which he captured; and in order to do this they have to conclude that Josephus gave the same denomination, Akra, to both the upper and lower cities; but if so, why does he not say that David *called* the upper city Akra?

The apparent explanation of Josephus is this: King David took the lower city with its citadel, Akra (Zion), and joined them together in one, so that together they formed the hill of Akra: afterwards, when the upper city was walled in, David called it the fortress (φρούριον).

Again we have:

1 *Maccabees* i. 30, 34.—He fell suddenly upon the city and smote it very sore. And when he had taken the spoils of the city, he set it on fire, and pulled down the houses and walls thereof on every side. Now builded they the city of David with a great and strong wall and with mighty towers, and it became a stronghold [an Akra] for them. And they put therein wicked men, and it became a place to lie in wait against the sanctuary..

The corresponding passage of Josephus gives it as follows:

Ant., xii. 5, § 4.—' When he [Antiochus] had pillaged the whole city, he burnt down the finest buildings, and when he had overthrown the city walls he built a stronghold [an Akra] in the lower city; for the place was higher and overlooked the

Temple, on which account he fortified it with high walls and towers, and put into it a garrison of Macedonians, and the impious and wicked part of the (Jewish) multitude dwelt in it.'

There are many other reasons against the upper city being the citadel, the Akra, which Josephus described David as having captured. For example, he speaks of Jerusalem and the city of David as one, and of the citadel as if it were merely a citadel; but the upper city appears to be at least four times as large as the lower city, and it is absurd to suppose a city occupying one-fourth the space of its own citadel; and again, Josephus makes David join the citadel on to the lower city; but if the lower city were only one-fourth of the citadel, surely he would have said that David joined the lower city on to the citadel. Then, again, Josephus appears to call the lower city Jerusalem, the city of David, and he says David built his palace there, and made buildings round about it. It thus appears that Josephus, though speaking more vaguely, is strictly in accord with the historical books and the 1 Maccabees. The only question that appears to remain is a question of degree: whether the citadel, Akra, which David captured, is not Millo of the city of David, and whether the lower city of Josephus is not Zion. As Akra was taken in and formed one with the lower city, so Millo may have been taken in and formed one with Zion.

Let us now pass on a step, and test Josephus as to the topography of his own time or a couple of centuries before it, viz., from the death of Simon Maccabeus; for it appears that it is only after that time that he can be looked up to as chief and almost the only authority. We now find* at once a change; he is no longer vague and general in his remarks, he is master of the field, and must write with precision, not only because he is almost the only historian of his time, but also because he is speaking of a city the topography of which was known to himself and to many who were likely to be his readers. We may, then, suppose that Josephus's account becomes valuable just when it is most wanted, viz., after the death of Simon Maccabeus.

We have then in this part shown a general agreement between the various topographical accounts of Jerusalem, which is not to be obtained by any other disposition of the various places mentioned; and we have now a secure basis on which the topography of the Holy City can be established.

The local indications which supplied this argument will be pointed out under the heads of 'The Temple' and 'The Tomb.'

* See Parts II., III., and IV.

PART II.

THE TOMB.

(Substance of a Lecture read before the Royal Historical Society.)

'There shall come out of Sion the Deliverer.'

THE subject on which we are to speak this evening is one upon which volumes have been written, and about which there is still much divergence of opinion; it is not possible to treat it exhaustively in the short space of time which can be devoted to the reading of an evening. It is only practicable to endeavour to lay aside the sophistries which surround the subject, and to put before you the outlines in as sharp relief as is consistent with their nature, leaving you subsequently to fill in the intervals as your own knowledge will best enable you.

In doing this I shall not attempt to confuse the subject by the supposition that there are alleged rival sites claiming attention. The site of the Holy Sepulchre has sustained the violent attacks made a few years ago upon its authenticity without damage to its reputation, and there is now a general concurrence of facts, historical, archæological, traditional, in favour of its having been the spot selected by the Emperor Constantine for the erection of the Church of the Resurrection, and there is great reason for supposing that the site he selected was the actual site of the Holy Sepulchre.

I throw over as utterly untenable the bold and original proposition of an enthusiastic writer, who in his zealous study of architecture in the East, has come to the remarkable conclusion that the Dome of the Rock is the Church of the Resurrection, and that the Sakhra of the Moslems is the Sepulchre of Christ; yet I shall from time to time cast a side-glance at this site of parallel holiness, where the temple of Solomon once stood, pointing out its condition at various periods; and I shall moreover show in Part IV. conclusively that the Sakhra under the Dome of the Rock, the site of Solomon's temple, cannot possibly be identified as the site of the Holy Sepulchre.

Starting with the assumption that the present site of the Holy Sepulchre is that which witnessed the crucifixion, sepulture, and resurrection, I shall proceed to point out how all evidence concurs in support, especially our most recent evidence, the excavations at Jerusalem.

The history of the Holy Sepulchre extends over five* epochs, viz.:

1. From the crucifixion, A.D. 33, to the recovery of the site by the Emperor Constantine, A.D. 325.

* George Williams, 'Holy City,' vol. ii., p. 136.

2. From the dedication of the Church of the Martyrdom, A.D. 336, to the destruction of it by Chosroes the Persian, A.D. 615.
3. From its restoration by the Patriarch-Vicar Modestus, A.D. 629, to its second destruction by the mad Fatimite Khalif of Cairo, El Hakim, A.D. 1010.
4. From its restoration by the Patriarch Nicephorus, A.D. 1048 (including its additions, A.D. 1120, by the Crusaders), to its destruction by fire, A.D. 1808.
5. From its restoration by the Greeks, A.D. 1810, to the present day.

Previous, however, to the consideration of the historical account, it is necessary to go back some years before the Christian era, and examine the ground as it originally existed; we shall thus be enabled to understand the configuration of the city of the Jebusites, and trace its changes to the time of the Romans, and we may comprehend how exactly the present site of the Holy Sepulchre suits the requirements of the case.

In doing this, I have not only the assistance of the many works which have been written on the subject during the last few years, but also the results of our underground researches, which have not hitherto been worked out, as regards the Holy Sepulchre.

I shall examine the subject from a new point of view, although in this particular instance arriving at old results, viz., the authenticity of the site of the Holy Sepulchre;* and I take this opportunity of asserting that I have arrived at a solution of the many difficulties surrounding the topography of Jerusalem, allowing in a great measure, or even entirely, of the reconciliation of all the ancient accounts to which credence has hitherto been given, and this without finding it necessary to omit, transfer, or modify any of the details in the manner which has hitherto been found requisite by others in order to bring about harmony.

This solution hinges upon the position I have assigned to Zion (discussed in 'The Parallel Holiness of Zion and Moriah'), a position which I contend is the only one suitable to the requirements of the narrative given in Holy Writ and the account of Josephus. In order to explain the position of this site, it is necessary to describe the position of the Holy City in early times.

The whole of the hill country about Jerusalem is of a very hard, rocky nature, elevated about 2,500 feet above the level of the Mediterranean Sea. Originally these hills were covered over with a layer of red earth from two to three feet thick. When, therefore, I produce a contoured plan of the rock levels about Jerusalem, I exhibit a plan of the ground as it existed in early days, less any cuttings or

* Which stands on the north-western hill of Jerusalem, on a portion of Mount Zion.

excavations of the rock which may have subsequently taken place.

This plan as now exhibited (Plate I.) has been made from observations gained during the excavations, and also from rock-levels obtained during the building of houses, and it will be at once apparent from inspection of it, that the rocky site about the Jebus of the ancients, with its precipitous hills and deep valleys, presents a very different aspect at the present day, when the valleys are filled up, in some cases to heights of a hundred feet or more, with millions of cubic yards of *débris* or rubbish. From this contoured plan it will be seen that this ancient site then consisted of three principal hills, to east, north-west, and south-west, separated by deep valleys.

All authorities, however much they may differ in other matters, unanimously concur in believing that the eastern hill is that which supported the Temple of the Jews, the outer walls of which still stand out of the filled-up valleys, and can be examined by all observers. It is commonly called Mount Moriah, though only once so called in the Bible.

All authorities are equally agreed that the hill to the south-west is the 'Upper City' of Josephus, and it follows that the hill to the north-west is the 'Lower City' of Josephus, or the Akra, so often mentioned by that historian as the third hill. The details of the proof that this hill to north-west is the Lower City, or Akra, are to be found in 'The Parallel Holiness of

Zion and Moriah.' Now, Josephus informs us that the Akra used to dominate the Temple entrance, and gave so much trouble to the Jews, visiting the Temple from the Upper City, during the time of the Macedonian occupation, that the Maccabees, on gaining possession, by working day and night for three years, succeeded in reducing the height of the Akra to such an extent that it ceased to be above the Temple mount.

The words of Josephus (Ant., xii. v. 4) regarding this matter are as follows :

'And when he had overthrown the city walls, he built a citadel (or Akra) in the Lower City, for the place was high, and overlooked the Temple, on which account he fortified it with high walls and towers, and put into it a garrison of Macedonians.' Ant., xii. ix. 3 : 'At this time it was that the garrison in the citadel (or Akra) at Jerusalem, with the Jewish runagates, did a great deal of harm to the Jews, for the soldiers that were in that garrison rushed out upon the sudden, and destroyed such as were going up to the Temple in order to offer their sacrifices, for this Akra adjoined to and overlooked the Temple.' Ant., xiii. vi. 7 : 'Simon overthrew the city Gazara, and Joppa, and Jamnia. He also took the Akra of Jerusalem by siege, and cast it to the ground, that it might not be any more a place of refuge to their enemies when they took it, to do them a mischief, as it had been until now. And when he had done this, he thought it their best way, and most for their advantage, to level the very mountain itself on which the Akra happened to stand, that so the Temple might be higher than it ... so they all set themselves to work, and levelled the mountain, and in that work spent both day and night without intermission, which cost them three whole years before it was removed, and brought to an entire level with the plain of the rest of the city. After which the Temple was the highest of all the buildings; now the Akra, as well as the mountain on which it stood, were demolished.'

In order to obtain the true appearance of this third hill as it once stood, it is, therefore, necessary to add on to the plan the contours of the portions of rock cut away by the Maccabees. This I have attempted to do. The first result is to find a want supplied in the present features of the rock contours. The scarps to the west of the Tyropœon, bounding the Upper City, will now be found to bound the Lower City also.

Secondly, it will be found that this rocky Mount of Akra is now naturally by far the strongest of the three hills for defensive purposes, and is, I contend, the original site of the fortress of Jebus, Mount Zion, the Akra of the Septuagint.

This position I have assigned to Zion is the only one which allows of accord in the several accounts, and is the only site yet proposed which will render intelligible the passage: 'Now after this he (Manasseh) built a wall without the city of David, on the west side of Gihon in the valley, even to the entering in at the fish gate.'

Around this Zion (formerly Jebus) a wall originally

existed, which Josephus informs us King David, on his occupation, connected with the Phrourion or Upper City, which hitherto had been a suburb, extending it completely round the latter; and Solomon in a succeeding generation added in the hill of the Temple, Mount Moriah.

Now, turning to the map, it will be seen (if the contours are examined) that for purposes of defence, the west wall of the ancient Zion, as extended by King David, would have run in a particular direction, which I can only indicate by mentioning existing sites. It would have run down south, along the site where Khan ez Zeit now stands, past the remains of the old portico (of which mention will hereafter be made), until it met the northern scarp of the Upper City, after crossing the deep Tyropœon, which here runs from west to east.

This passage of the valley by the wall connecting Zion to the Upper City would naturally be the weak point in the defence of the combined new city, and as Gihon in the valley (Tyropœon), now represented by the modern Pool of Hezekiah, or Birket Hammam, was situated at the upper end of the valley, near the neck joining the Upper City to Zion, the reasons why King Manasseh should have built a wall on the west side of Gihon in the valley are very obvious. He did so in order to strengthen the defences, and to cover a weak point.

These circumstances account satisfactorily for the re-entering angle in the city wall to the north-west

SKETCH OF JERUSALEM AT TIME OF VESPASIAN.

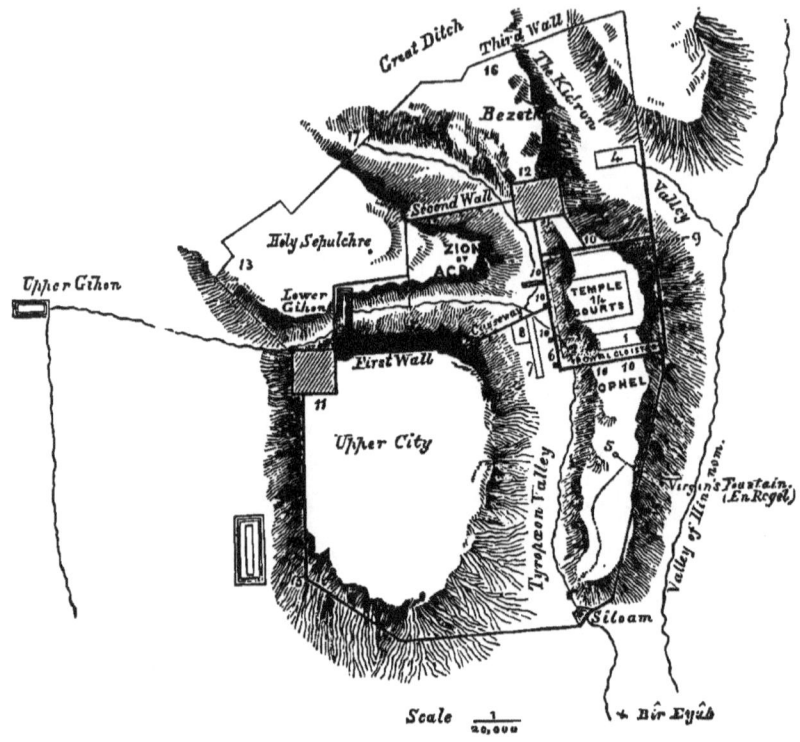

of the city, where the Church of the Holy Sepulchre now stands, the existence of which has presented a difficulty to many who have studied the subject.

As time wore on, the large Upper City became covered with houses, and rivalled Mount Zion; and after the building of the Temple, and consequent removal of the ark, the Upper City became the more important, until at last, during the wars of the Jews, Simon Maccabæus saw the great inconvenience of having three forts at Jerusalem, viz., the Akra, the Upper City, and the Temple; and consequently he cut down the Akra, or Zion; and thus the Upper City became the citadel of Jerusalem, 'being the highest and more direct.'

Subsequently when King Herod fortified Jerusalem, the Upper City became the citadel surrounded by the first wall; the second wall was built on the lines of the old wall round Zion.

Some ten years after the crucifixion the third wall was built, enclosing the site of the Holy Sepulchre and the suburbs north of Zion.

We may now view the plan of the city as it existed in the time of Pilate; an indented wall bounding the northern portion; the site of the Holy Sepulchre being in the re-entering angle *without* the wall, past which ran the main thoroughfare from Jerusalem to Jaffa and Cæsarea.

Thus having cursorily glanced at the general appearance of the walls around the site, I will refer to the site itself.

It is worthy of mention that the walls of the present Church of the Holy Sepulchre, which in all probability stand on the lines of the former walls, are built square with the west wall of the Haram area, that old wall ascribed to the time of Herod ; it is further to be remarked that a line, drawn from a point a few feet north of the Holy Sepulchre, perpendicular to the old west wall of the Haram area, passes through the remains of the portico (ascribed to Constantine) still existing in the market street, and runs straight down one of the principal thoroughfares, the Akabât at Takiyeh, to the gate of the Inspector in the Haram area.

It may be naturally inferred from this that this street existed when the site of the Holy Sepulchre was first built over by Constantine, and that advantage of the position was taken to give his portico one of the finest prospects that could be desired, a view upon and over the Temple area, and up to the Mount of Olives.

This street is in many parts cut in the rock, and appears to be one of the old streets of Jerusalem. If so, it would from its position have been the principal thoroughfare from the Antonia, Temple, and market of the Lower City to Jaffa and Cæsarea. The city gate would have stood where Constantine's portico was afterwards built and now remains, and the thoroughfare beyond the wall would have passed close to the present site of the crucifixion.

At the present day the place of public execution at

Jerusalem is just outside the principal gate, the Jaffa gate, and so no doubt it was in former days outside the then principal gate, for then, as now, public executions took place outside the city wall, near a public road or other conspicuous spot. We are told that the crucifixion took place without the city, yet nigh to the city. The site so far accords, for it is a hundred and twenty yards without the west wall, and eighty yards beyond the north wall: the Holy Sepulchre being forty yards north-west by west of Golgotha. Moreover the site fully comes within the law stated by Lightfoot, that nobody was to be buried within fifty cubits of a town.

Now regarding objections that have been raised against this site having been used for executions and for sepulture at the time of the crucifixion. In the first place it has been urged that as this portion was walled in by Agrippa a few years after the crucifixion, the presumption is that at that time it was a populous suburb, and could not have been used for burial purposes. This proposition, however, cannot be maintained, for the wall of Agrippa was built for strategic purposes, and the interior may or may not have been populated so far as the building of the wall is concerned; the wall being required because the northern front of Jerusalem had lost its strength by the cutting down of Akra or Zion under the Maccabees, and presented but a poor defence to the Roman battering-rams. Moreover, Josephus tells us that the space enclosed by the third wall was but sparsely populated, and also that both Cestius and Titus camped within the walls, which they could not have done had the space been extensively occupied by houses. The second objection is that tombs were not permitted within the walls of a city. To this there is the reply that this site was not brought within the walls until *after* the date of the crucifixion, and besides we know from Josephus that somewhere near this site was the tomb of the High Priest John, within the third wall. And again we have existing at the present day other undoubtedly ancient Jewish tombs (those of Nicodemus, etc.), close to the Holy Sepulchre.

It is true that at one time there was a feeble attempt made by those who do not believe in the site of the Holy Sepulchre, to prove that these tombs were forgeries; but this attempt proved abortive, as these tombs were known many centuries before any doubt was cast upon the authenticity of the site of the Holy Sepulchre, and few can imagine persons excavating tombs in the rock many hundred years ago, merely in order that they might prevent doubts that have only arisen during the present century.

Lastly, there is a supposed difficulty on account of the place of sepulture and place of execution being so close together, it being argued that a person of the social status of Joseph of Arimathea would not have excavated his tomb so near a place of public execution. The distance, however, is not so excessively close, for there is a space of forty yards between Golgotha and the Holy Sepulchre, which in the suburbs of so populous a city as Jerusalem, where no doubt each plot of ground was of high value, may be considered not too close for the requirements. Besides, do not our own records themselves allude to the propinquity of the two? 'In the place where He was crucified there was a garden, and in the garden a new sepulchre.'

Again, other forms of objection have been raised. It has been assumed that the sepulchre of our Lord would have raised no feeling of interest in Christians, Jews, or Romans in early days, and that therefore the site would have been lost. Now, as regards Christians, we cannot suppose that they were all of that simple, earnest faith they were enjoined to attain to, and it is absurd to suppose that all the earliest Christians were enabled, by embracing a new faith, to divest their minds permanently of veneration for sites rendered holy by the presence, during life, of the founder of their religion, more especially as we are aware that in the fourth century an excessive veneration for such sites obtained among Christians. We cannot doubt that in the earliest days, as now, there were those whose minds were so constituted or shaped that they could not resist giving a passing thought at times to the 'tomb in which He had been laid,' of which the angel, after the resurrection, said, 'He is risen, He is not here; *behold the place* where they laid Him.'

It seems probable that from the first the site of the Holy Sepulchre was known among the Christians, and that it has never been forgotten. As regards the Romans, within the province, it is impossible to suppose that they looked upon the crucifixion of our Lord simply as an ordinary occurrence. The Jews were a turbulent race, swarming over the countries of the Levant, and the Romans understood the art of governing foreign populations far too well to omit noticing the emotion and excitement which prevailed amongst the Jews during our Lord's ministry, and they would without doubt have taken ample memoranda of all that occurred, and have forwarded them to head-quarters.

The statement of early writers that the site was defiled by a temple and statue of Venus is itself sufficient to show that the Holy Sepulchre was an object of veneration and attraction to the early Christians, for the Romans are shown to have treated it as they did other holy places, such as the Temple of Jerusalem and that of Gerizim, on both of which sites they erected temples to the gods of the Latins, either out of derision or else, and more probably, in order to induce the pilgrims to these sites gradually to adopt the polytheism of Rome.

On the other hand, some have supposed that the site of the Holy Sepulchre may have been ascertained by Constantine from the plans the Romans made in the first century. This is possible, but it seems much more probable that the site was known from concurrent tradition, and marked by the Temple of Venus, which will be mentioned hereafter.

These questions, however, lead directly to the early history of the Holy Sepulchre, of which there is very little information to be obtained until the fourth century, when two witnesses give us concurrent testimony on the subject, viz., Eusebius, Bishop of Cæsarea, and the Bordeaux Pilgrim.

Eusebius, who wrote at various times between the years 315 and 338, was living in Palestine at the time that the recovery of the Holy Sepulchre took place, and was present at the dedication of the Church of the Resurrection, A.D. 336.

He admits us to a retrospective glimpse of events in stating that the Emperor Constantine, inspired with a divine impulse, determined to recover the Holy Sepulchre of our Lord, which certain impious persons had formerly endeavoured to consign to oblivion, and who for this purpose had brought together a great quantity of earth, and had filled and levelled up the place until they had concealed the cave, and had them paved over with stone, and erected thereon a temple to Venus. There is reason to suppose that this was done in the reign of the Emperor Hadrian, and that at the same time a temple to Jupiter was erected on the sister site of holiness, the rock on which the Temple of Solomon had stood. That a temple to Venus did exist at Jerusalem in or near the time of Hadrian, is evident from a coin of the reign of Antoninus Pius, his successor, which has a figure of Venus represented standing in a temple, with the legend C.A.C. This account of Eusebius tends to show that at this early period the sepulchre of our Lord was accounted holy ; but whatever may have been the motives of the impious persons in covering over the sepulchre and erecting thereon a temple to Venus, there can be no doubt that the actual result was to keep the rock intact during a great number of years until the advent of a Christian emperor.

The account given by Eusebius of the removal of the temple to Venus is as follows :

iii. 27.—' Nor did the emperor's zeal stop here ; but he gave further orders, that the materials of what was thus destroyed, both stone and timber, should be removed, and thrown as far from the spot as possible, and this command was also speedily executed. . . . Nay more, fired with holy ardour, he directed that the ground itself should be dug to a considerable depth, and the soil which had been polluted by the foul impurities of demon-worship, transplanted to a far-distant place.'

iii. 28.—' This also was accomplished without delay. But as soon as the original surface of the ground, beneath the covering of the earth, appeared, immediately, and contrary to all expectation, the venerable and hallowed monument of our Saviour's resurrection was discovered. Then, indeed, did this most holy cave present a faithful similitude to His return to life, in that, after lying buried in darkness, it again emerged to light, and afforded to all who came to witness the sight a clear and visible proof of the wonders of which that spot had once been the scene, a testimony to the resurrection of the Saviour clearer than any voice could give.'

Before proceeding further, it is desirable to devote a few words to a study of the configuration of the ground about the Holy Sepulchre.

The shape of the numerous existing Jewish rock-cut tombs at Jerusalem is now so well known, that I will not linger over a description. Advantage was usually taken of a natural scarp on the side of a quarry, or else the rock was scarped down for the purpose, and an entrance was made to the proposed tomb in the face of the upright cliff. This entrance generally led into a vestibule, from the three sides of which openings led into three square-cut chambers, and in the sides of these chambers again the kokim, or places for the bodies, were cut. Thus a full-sized tomb would have three chambers, with nine to eleven kokim in each. In many, however, there is only one chamber, with nine kokim. In some cases benches have been cut out on each side of the chamber, in which case there would only be accommodation for three bodies.

That the so-called tomb of Nicodemus is of the Jewish type there can be no doubt, and it has been recently proved satisfactorily that it consisted of a chamber with three kokim on each side. The question then arises as to whether the adjoining Holy Sepulchre was also a kok. That this may have been so, has been alleged in a paper on the Holy Sepulchre ('P.E.F. Quarterly,' July, 1877); but I am myself inclined to think that it was a single tomb, lying in a recess*

---

* See St. John xx. 12.

parallel to the side of the chamber, and not perpendicular to it as the kokim are.

Whatever shape, however, the interior of the tomb assumed, the entrance would have been in the same style in either case, and was in all probability cut in the side of the cliff facing east, which at the present day (from having been cut still further back) rises to the north-west of the church of the Holy Sepulchre.

The original object of this scarp is only obvious when the place is examined. The ground rises gently to the north-west from the wall of the city; it would be necessary therefore to cut it down for some yards to the front of the wall. The stones from this cutting would serve for the wall of the city. The levelled space would serve for the garden about Golgotha, an isolated knoll of hard rock; and the scarp of the quarry would be used for the tombs of the wealthy. With this configuration of the ground in view, the account of Eusebius can readily be understood.

As far as the tomb itself is concerned, all that was then done was to cut it out from the rocky cliff so as to pave the open space around the tomb to serve as a sanctum, with cloisters on the north, west, and south; but there was no church or covering built over the tomb, and it was open to the sky until the reconstruction, A.D. 629. The great basilica of Constantine was erected to the east of the Holy Sepulchre, rectangular with atrium and portal, reaching up to the west wall of the city and through the wall, so that the church situated outside the walls was entered from the market-place within the city.

The account is as follows : *

'First he adorned the sacred cave itself, as the chief part of the whole work, and the hallowed monument at which the angel, radiant with light, had once declared to all that regeneration which was first manifested in the Saviour's person. This monument, therefore, as the chief part of the whole, the emperor's zealous magnificence beautified with rare columns, and profusely enriched with the most splendid decorations of every kind.

'The next object of his attention was a space of ground of great extent, and open to the pure air of heaven. This he adorned with a pavement of finely-polished stone, and enclosed it on three sides with porticoes of great length. At the side opposite to the sepulchre, which was the east side, the church itself was erected; a noble work rising to a great height and of great extent both in length and breadth. The interior of this structure was floored with marble slabs of various colours, while the external surface of the walls, which shone with polished stone exactly fitted together, exhibited a degree of splendour in no respect inferior to that of marble. With regard to the roof, it was covered on the outside with lead, as a protection against the rains of winter. But the inner part of the roof, which was finished with sculptured fretwork, extended in a series of connected compartments like a vast sea over the whole church ; and being overlaid throughout with the purest gold, caused the entire building to glitter, as it were, with

* Vide 'Jerusalem,' p. 59.

rays of light. * Besides this were two porticoes on each side with upper and lower ranges of pillars, corresponding in length with the church itself, and these had also their roofs ornamented with gold. Of these porticoes, those which were exterior to the church were supported by columns of great size, while those within rested on piles of stone beautifully adorned on the surface. Three gates placed exactly east, were intended to receive those who entered the church.

'Opposite to these gates the crowning part of the whole was the hemisphere, which rose to the very summit of the church. This was encircled by twelve columns (according to the number of the apostles of our Saviour), having their capitals embellished with silver bowls of great size, which the emperor himself presented as a splendid offering to his God.

'In the next place he enclosed the atrium, which occupied the space leading to the entrance in front of the church. This comprehended, first, the court; then the porticoes on each side; and lastly, the gates of the court. After these, in the midst of the open market-place, the entrance-gates, of the whole work, which were of exquisite workmanship, afforded to passers-by on the outside a view of the interior, which could not fail to excite astonishment.'

There is a difficult passage in the account of Eusebius above, relating to this basilica, which is also translated as follows:

* 'Moreover on either side, double piers of double porticoes above and below ground, extending the full length of the Temple.'

---

* The passage has thus different meanings in the two translations. The second is adopted by Mr. Fergusson.

THE TOMB.   49

We know that the rock in Khan ez Zeit, where is the remnant of the portico opening from the Martyrion upon the city, is only about eight feet below the floor of the Holy Sepulchre, and that the floor of the so-called chapel of Helena is about fourteen feet below the Holy Sepulchre; it seems probable therefore that there was a descent from the great eastern portico into the basilica, and then an ascent again to the Holy Sepulchre court.

Eusebius particularly mentions that the rock around the tomb was cut out in a 'level land,' implying that the ground was quarried level from the city wall.

The Martyrion was completed and dedicated, A.D. 335, two years after the visit of the Bordeaux Pilgrim, whose account is of value, inasmuch as it clearly proves that at that time the Holy Sepulchre was in the position it is now found, and not in any other part of the city.

He passed through the Temple Sanctuary on Mount Moriah, and saw on the site of the Temple two statues (of the time of Hadrian) in front of the temple already alluded to as having been erected to Jupiter (this is all mentioned by Dion). He then ascended to Sion (the Upper City),* and having visited various localities, then passed through the first wall surrounding the Upper City on the north towards the Nablous gate; on his left he saw the little knoll of Golgotha, where our Lord was crucified, and within a stone's throw was the sepulchre, near which at that time the Emperor Constantine was erecting a basilica.

* Vide page 22.

St. Cyril, who was born in Palestine A.D. 315, and visited or lived in Jerusalem A.D. 334, describes the Martyrion A.D. 347, and refers to the tomb as having been cut by Constantine so as to stand out from the rock; and Jerome, who lived at Bethlehem A.D. 400, gives evidence to the same effect.

Whether the rock-cut tomb still exists within the marble casing of the Holy Sepulchre, is not a material question so far as the authenticity of the site is concerned, for it is certain from the nature of the ground that rock once existed where the sepulchre now stands, and we know that during the middle ages both the emissaries of the mad Hakim and other fanatics attempted to remove the rock-cut tomb, and may have partially succeeded. It is asserted, however, that rock has been seen as forming part of the sepulchre at various periods, notably in A.D. 1558, by Boniface of Ragusa, when the whole of the sepulchre was laid bare. In A.D. 1868, I sent to England a portion of the rocky floor.

Eusebius, in speaking of the position of the Holy Sepulchre, states that Constantine erected his basilica in the midst of the city of Jerusalem, apparently referring to its having been within the line of the third wall, and so near the second wall bounding Mount Zion or Akra, on which David's palace once stood, and facing the market-place. In another passage he tells us that around the Holy Sepulchre was built the new Jerusalem, facing towards that which became so infamous in the time of our Lord, and was consequently brought to desolation, evidently referring to the Upper City, which faces the Akra, and which in the days of Herod contained his palaces.

All subsequent testimony is in accordance with the statements of Eusebius regarding the position of the Holy Sepulchre, and there is no possibility of there having been any transference of the site after the building of the Martyrion by Constantine.

It is not until the fifth century that we have any detailed account of the manner in which the site of the Holy Sepulchre was recovered in the time of Constantine, and then all writers concur in stating that it was Helena, the aged mother of Constantine, who made the discovery by divine intimation.

They relate that when she came to Jerusalem, she made inquiries carefully among the inhabitants, and after a long and onerous search discovered the Holy Sepulchre, and near it three crosses, with the inscription written by order of Pilate, which however was not attached to any of the crosses. Being unable to determine which was the true cross, the Bishop Macarius proposed the usual test. A noble lady of Jerusalem lay ill of an incurable disease; the three crosses were presented to her in succession. The first two produced no effect; but at the approach of the third she opened her eyes, recovered her health, and sprang out of bed in perfect health.

It is probable that it was the pious Helena who induced her son Constantine to search for the sepulchre, and to adorn it and build the Martyrion,

4—2

that during his lifetime his flatterers ascribed the work entirely to him, but that after his death the pious writers gave her credit not only for her own work, but also for what Constantine himself had done.

During the period that intervened between the date of the erection of the Martyrion and the commencement of the seventh century, Jerusalem became the grand centre of attraction to the whole Christian world.

Pilgrims, in increasing numbers, year by year, flocked to the Holy City from all parts of Christendom, and Palestine became the home of hundreds of monasteries, its caves the habitation of hermits, and its mountain-sides pierced with cells.

These might have been quiet days for the Christians had they kept up to their original standard of faith; but the Church which had survived oppression and wrong, or rather had owing thereto kept up a sturdy vitality, now in its palmy days succumbed to the enervating influence of luxury and sloth, and rapidly became an asylum for those who were Christians but in name.

Add to this, the episcopal thrones were filled by hermits and monks who had either lost their freedom of mind by the slavery of monastic discipline, or had assumed the garb as a step to those much sought-for appointments, having learnt by observation the secret paths which led to their possession. Thus in the Church bribery and corruption reigned supreme, and battles and strife continually disturbed the peace of the Holy City, until the measure of its cup was full, a terrible vengeance overtook the unfortunate Christians, and the local Church, bathed in blood, became subject to a tyranny and thraldom from which it has, up to the present time, only at intervals temporarily been able to emancipate itself.

This Nemesis overtook the Christians A.D. 615, when Heraclius reigned over the Eastern Empire, and Zachariah was Bishop of Jerusalem.

Chosroes II., King of Persia, with his hordes, swept over the boundary of the empire, taking city after city, until he rested at Damascus; thence urged by the religious prejudices of the Magi, he resolved to attempt the conquest of Jerusalem, an act which his grandfather, Nurshervan, had meditated upon before him.

The position which Jerusalem at this time held in the Christian world may be gathered from the relentless spirit of the Magi, who since the time of Artaxerxes had given themselves over to the most rigid persecution of rival sects whenever they obtained an opportunity, and who now that they were in power would be content with nothing less than the destruction of the Holy City.

Strange to say, this was accomplished by the aid of the Jews, for this much-persecuted race, having recently revolted and having been severely punished by the emperor, saw with unbounded enthusiasm the unchecked progress of the Persian hordes over the frontier of the Eastern Empire, and they flocked to the standard of Chosroes in great numbers.

In their exultation they formed the idea of issuing

from the several cities, and suddenly appearing before the Holy City at Easter, in order to capture it by surprise; but the news of the conspiracy reached the ears of the Christians, and before their object could be accomplished the bishop had closed the gates of the city, and had imprisoned a great number of the more wealthy Jews.

The insurgent Jews arrived before the closely-barricaded Holy City, and commenced destroying the suburbs, together with the suburban Christian churches. It is related that as each church outside was destroyed, the Christians within the city struck off the heads of one hundred Jews and rolled them over the city walls; but this retaliation had no effect upon the enthusiastic insurgents: church after church was demolished until twenty thousand Jewish heads had been cast down the outer slopes of the city.

The insurgents, however, found that enthusiasm alone was not sufficient in the attack upon a walled city; they could effect no lodgment within. And hearing of Chosroes's advance, they returned to augment his forces, which had already been reinforced by twenty-six thousand Jews from Galilee of unsurpassed bigotry, a province then, as now, teeming with fanaticism among all religious sects.

In one united body advanced the worshippers of Jehovah and the votaries of Fire, to jointly attack and destroy the Holy City of the Christians, which had so often in former days been gallantly defended by the sons of Abraham.

The city attempted but little defence against so strong a force, and capitulated at once, submitting most pusillanimously to a fearful penalty.

The Christians were ruthlessly slain to the number of ninety thousand of both sexes and all ages. The Jews and Magi had ample opportunity for wreaking their vengeance upon their disarmed antagonists, and they did not stint themselves : the churches of Gethsemane were first destroyed, and then with a great part of the city were demolished the basilica of Constantine, the churches of Calvary and Holy Sepulchre—the two latter being burnt to the ground. All the rich votive offerings of three hundred years were gathered together and carried back to Persia, together with the wood of the true cross, and the Patriarch Zachariah was also carried away a captive. Fortunately for the patriarch, the wife of Chosroes was a Christian, and she, by her intercession, procured for him good treatment, and also the preservation of the wood of the true cross.

As objections have been made to the fact that the churches about the holy places were destroyed, it will be interesting to examine the views taken by several writers on the subject.

Gibbon tells us : ' The sepulchre of Christ, and the stately churches of Helena and Constantine, were consumed, or at least damaged by the flames.'

Milman states : ' Every Christian church was demolished ; that of the Holy Sepulchre was the great object of furious hatred ; the stately building of

Helena and Constantine was abandoned to the flames.'

Besant gives: 'The church of the Holy Sepulchre— *i.e.* what Eusebius calls, speaking of it as a whole, the Temple, the basilica with its porticoes and pillars, and the decorations of the sepulchre, were all destroyed.'

Robinson's view is: 'The splendid churches were thrown down, and that of the Holy Sepulchre burned with fire.'

There appears to be a general concurrence in the view that there was a total destruction of the buildings of Constantine by the Persians in the year A.D. 614, and that when the restoration took place, there were many modifications of the original design.

Palestine remained now for some years under the Persian yoke, which however appears to have been but nominal, for during the enforced absence of Zachariah, we learn that the Patriarch-Vicar Modestus was furnished by the Patriarch of Alexandria with a large sum of money for the purpose of rebuilding the churches of the Resurrection, of Calvary, and also a church of the Assumption. Whether in his reconstruction he altered the general plan from the original to any very great extent cannot now be ascertained; but it seems that he made several alterations, and covered over the cloisters about the Holy Sepulchre with a dome. It is evident from the account of Arculf that several alterations were made.

Fifteen years elapsed before the Emperor of the

East was able to turn back the arms of the Persians, and cause their monarch to sue for peace from within his own capital. Then when Egypt and Syria had again returned to the rule of their former master, Heraclius, after celebrating his triumph at Constantinople with much splendour, came to Jerusalem in the year 629, carrying with him on his shoulders the true cross, which had remained intact during its sojourn in Persia, the seals of the chest in which it was packed having remained unbroken. This, the last appearance of the Emperor of the East in Jerusalem, was made memorable by a merciless and bloody persecution of the Jews (in retaliation for their recent revengeful excesses); to this he was instigated by the more fanatical Christians. Henceforward the mutual intolerance between these rival sects frequently burst all bounds, resulting in fearful persecutions, generally on the part of the Christians, they being the stronger; but the Jews, when occasion offered, have not been behindhand in showing a disposition to square up outstanding accounts with their antagonists.

This mutual hatred, which has now so happily and entirely died out of our own country, but which still exists in several countries of Europe, can yet be found growing stronger and stronger as we journey through Europe towards the East, until it may be found existing in its old form in many cities and villages of Palestine. At Jerusalem at the present day there is the strongest feeling of mutual dislike between the native Christians and Jews. This is at once apparent should, by any accident, a Jew, male or female, happen unwittingly to cross the plaza in front of the Holy Sepulchre. The Greeks state that they are in possession of a firman authorising them to beat any such offender, and whether they have or not, there can be no doubt that they exercise their asserted right in a most arbitrary manner.

The continued strife between the Byzantine and Persian potentates, tending in so great a degree to their mutual weakness, was watched with the greatest anxiety by the keen-sighted Mahomet, who perceived between their tottering powers a prospect of the aggrandisement of his own race. Born, A.D. 569, he did not become conspicuous to the outer world until A.D. 629, the very year in which, as has been stated, Heraclius entered Jerusalem in triumph and massacred the Jews, thereby undoing for the Christians any good moral effects they may have derived from their recent misfortunes, and reducing them again to their former state of mental servitude to unchristian feelings and thought. Very different changes were taking place in this same year (A.D. 629) at Mecca, where Mahomet was striving to the best of his unaided judgment to emancipate the Arabians from the fetters of idolatry by the removal of the three hundred and sixty idols at that focus of false gods, the Kaaba.

Mahomet at that time raised the little cloud which in the short space of one hundred years was to spread east and west over the land, from the East Indies to the Pillars of Hercules, forcing on the natives, both civilized and barbarous, the errors of that wonderful religion which he initiated, and which is now one of the most widespread religions of the world.

The progress of the Moslems was only temporarily checked by their founder's death; his lieutenants, ably carrying on their master's design, and gaining strength as they progressed, quickly swept over the confines of Arabia, and in a short time wrested from the Emperor Heraclius the provinces of Palestine and Egypt, which he had so recently regained from the Persians. The enervated host of Persia itself soon succumbed to the victorious Moslems, whose motto was 'Victory or Paradise.'

It is related that during ten years of Omar's administration, no less than thirty-six thousand cities and castles were captured, and ten thousand temples or churches demolished by the Moslems.

To these successful fanatics the city of Jerusalem presented a double attraction. First, it was to them a sacred city, containing the site of the Temple of the Jews, sanctified by the prophets, and more particularly by Mahomet himself, who ascended to heaven from the sacred rock in the Haram area during his celebrated midnight journey from Mecca, and who even originally made this rock the Moslem Kibleh, or turning-point in prayer, though he afterwards gave preference to the Kaaba at Mecca.

Secondly, it was an attraction as containing the

Kaaba of the Christian world, the Holy Sepulchre, the acquisition of which by the Moslems would put the Christians to a disadvantage.

Although the Moslems revere their Prophet Isa (Jesus Christ) as the greatest prophet after Mahomet, and indeed in some measure give his a higher rank, in a confused manner, and although they highly revere the tombs of their prophets (as, for example, the so-called tomb of Sitti Mariam, the Blessed Virgin, in the Kedron Valley), yet they could have no feeling except that of repugnance for the Holy Sepulchre, as to them, if genuine, it would only be the tomb of a criminal. For one of their bitterest accusations against the Christians is on account of their affirming that their Prophet Isa was crucified, the Moslems believing that so great a prophet could not have suffered so ignominious a death, and asserting that another man, a criminal, suffered in his place, while Isa ascended into heaven without feeling the sting of death.

It is necessary to realise this phase of thought in the mind of Moslems, in order to comprehend their feelings regarding the Holy Sepulchre. Had it been compatible with their religion to believe that their Prophet Isa did suffer death on the cross, then there is little doubt that they would have taken possession of the tomb, and have guarded it with the same jealousy as they guard those of their other prophets; to wit, the Cave of Macpelah, of David, of Nebi Musa, of Nebi Samwib, and others.

It was in the autumn of A.D. 636 that the Kaliph Omar sent his lieutenant, Abu Obeideh, to capture the Holy City; but though the army of Heraclius had melted away, and there was no extraneous help to be expected, the Patriarch Sophronius, governor of the city, energetically organised an army of citizens, and preparing for a resolute defence, sustained for four months the attacks of the ill-organised but daring soldiers of Islam.

When at last driven to seek terms, Sophronius expressed his determination to capitulate only to the Kaliph Omar in person; and Omar, feeling the importance of the prize now within his grasp, acceded to this request, and setting out from Medina arrived before Jerusalem, encamping on Olivet, where he was waited on by Sophronius, who was astonished at the stern simplicity with which the court of the Kaliph was conducted.

Omar in appearance seems to have differed little from the ordinary type of wandering Arab of the present day, and the patriarch, bowing low before him, and casting a glance at his uncouth figure and rough apparel, could not avoid muttering, 'Verily this is the abomination of desolation in the Holy Place.'

Omar insisted on being told the words of the patriarch, and accordingly a translation was made, which probably was somewhat modified as to its boldness, for Omar is recorded to have been pleased to hear that he was the subject of prophecy, as was

Alexander on a similar occasion nearly one thousand years before.

The Kaliph having arranged the terms of the capitulation, under which the Christians and Jews were to have freedom of worship and the use of their churches and synagogues, entered the gates of the city, followed by the Moslem army. It is stated that at this time there were in the city fifty thousand natives of Palestine, and twelve thousand Greeks.

Sophronius conducted Omar to the church of the Resurrection, and while there the latter expressed his wish to pray. The patriarch proposed that he should pray then and there, but Omar refused. The patriarch was then led to the basilica of Constantine, and a mat there spread for his devotions, but again he refused. Then going out to the eastern gate of the church, he prayed on the steps alone. After this he explained to the patriarch his reason for not having prayed in the church; had he done so, the Christians would have lost the right to the church, for the Moslems would have taken possession after his death, saying, 'There prayed Omar.'

Not satisfied even with this precaution, he gave the patriarch on a paper in writing a command that not more than one Moslem should pray on the steps at one time; that they should not be called to prayers there as they are at their own mosque. This act of Omar shows us that with his simplicity of life, there was also a conscientious desire to be just to his neighbour in a manner which redounds to his credit, and which must lead every Christian to honour him as a noble-minded man.

He now asked the patriarch for a site where he might build a place of prayer, according to the terms of the capitulation; and to this he was told that he could have the place on which the Grecian Emperor (Julian) failed to build, the rock which Jacob called the 'gate of heaven,' over which the Jews built the Holy of Holies, the centre of the earth, to which the Jews turn as a Kibleh, the morsel of Paradise from which Mahomet ascended to heaven. This rock for many years past, since the time of Julian, had remained covered with dung and rubbish.

Omar having performed his devotions at the tower of David near the Jaffa Gate, now asked to be shown the mosque of David, by which he meant the threshing-floor given to David as a site for the Temple Solomon afterwards built.

This led to a misunderstanding, for the patriarch supposed he alluded to Mount Zion on which David had worshipped, where the ark had stood; and accordingly conducted Omar again to the church of the Resurrection, saying 'This is the mosque of David.' A remark which shows that he was not unaware that the church of the Holy Sepulchre is built on the original Mount Zion.

Omar reflected a little, and then curtly replied to the patriarch, 'Thou liest!' He was then conducted to a church in the Upper City, the present Cœnaculum and tomb of David: to this he again objected, and it being understood what he was in search of, he was taken to the Sakhra itself in the Haram area, which he found defiled with dung. Over this rock, or near it, he appears to have built a wooden house of prayer, which is described by Arculf, who visited Jerusalem A.D. 680, or thereabout, the present dome of the rock having been built some years after by the Kaliph Abd el Melik, A.D. 688.

During the four centuries and a half which elapsed between the occupation of Jerusalem by the Moslems and the retreat before the victorious Crusaders, the church of the Holy Sepulchre experienced extreme vicissitudes, at one time the centre of attraction of Christendom, tolerated by Islam, and again deserted by the Christians, and ruthlessly pillaged by the Moslems. It was so frequently demolished and again restored that scarcely a trace remains visible above ground of the original buildings; but yet the accounts from age to age are so clear, and the alterations so progressive, that it is not difficult to perceive how the buildings of Constantine have gradually been removed and changed in plan to those existing at the present day.

The account given by Arculf, a French bishop who visited Jerusalem about A.D. 680, recorded by Adamnan, Abbot of Iona, gives a very clear description of the churches about the Holy Sepulchre, as they were restored, A.D. 629, by Modestus, after the demolition of the old buildings by Chosroes the Persian.

Most fortunately this account is accompanied by a plan, which, though not drawn to scale, has the appearance of having been a faithful representation, and corresponds in a marked degree to the plan of the existing church, so much so that the enthusiastic writer who, in order to support his views regarding the Dome of the Rock, suggests a transfer of the site from thence to the present site in the eighth or ninth century, has been obliged to propound the extraordinary proposition that the Crusaders must have built the present church from this plan of Arculf. There is not a tittle of evidence in favour of such a proposition; but the fact of its having been made serves to show how closely this plan of the seventh century must resemble that of the buildings of the existing church, even to the minds of those who reject the authenticity of the present site.

Arculf informs us that on the spot where the Temple once stood near the eastern wall of the Haram area, the Saracens had erected a square house of prayer in a rough manner, by raising planks and beams on old ruins, probably the remains of the Temple of Jupiter. From this and other considerations it is apparent that he visited Jerusalem previous to the building of the present Dome of the Rock by Abd el Melek, commenced A.D. 688, and completed A.D. 691.

Arculf's attention, however, was more particularly directed to the holy places of the Christians in Jerusalem itself. He found the Church of the

Resurrection very large and *round*, encompassed with three walls, with a broad space between each, containing three altars in middle wall on south, north, and west. Twelve stone columns of extraordinary magnitude supported the buildings, and through the three opposite walls were eight entrances, four to the south-east and four to the north-east.

In the middle space was a round grotto cut in the solid rock, the interior of which was large enough for nine men to pray standing. The entrance was from the east side, the sepulchre within on the northern side, raised three palms from the ground and seven feet in length, hewn out of the rock, which was not uniform in colour, but appeared to be a mixture of white and red. Internally the rock was visible all over, exhibiting the marks of the workman's tools; but externally, it was covered with choice marble to the very top of the roof.

South of the Church of the Resurrection was the square Church of the Virgin Mary; east of this was a large church over the rock of Golgotha; and again to the north-east was the basilica of Constantine, called the Martyrdom, erected on the spot where the true cross was found, two hundred and thirty-three years after it had been buried. It is thus evident that a considerable change had taken place in the construction of the buildings after the demolition of Chosroes, especially in the covering in of the open space around the Holy Sepulchre by the round Church of the Resurrection.

Although the churches of the Holy Sepulchre were pillaged and restored, burnt and rebuilt, thrice during the eighth and ninth centuries, it does not appear that any important change was made in the plan of their construction, for both Willibald, A.D. 786, and Bernard, A.D. 870, follow Arculf in their descriptions; indeed Bernard considers that the full description given by Bede (from Arculf) precludes the necessity of his enlarging upon the subject; and we may safely consider the churches to have remained substantially the same from the time of Modestus, A.D. 629, until their total destruction by El Hakim, the mad Fatimite Kaliph, A.D. 1010.

During the early portion of this period, the Christians appear to have been tolerated, if not respected, until near the close of the eighth century, when Palestine was desolated by civil war. Then Haroun ar Raschid came to the throne at Bagdad, and struck up a friendship with Charlemagne, the Emperor of the West, which resulted in the sending to Charlemagne the keys of the Holy Sepulchre, Calvary, which arrived at Rome at Christmas, A.D. 800, shortly previous to his coronation.

The Christians did not long enjoy the fruits of this good-will between these two great potentates, for during the discords which arose, A.D. 812, on the death of Haroun ar Raschid, their Church of the Holy Sepulchre was again ruined and profaned. On this occasion it was rebuilt by the Patriarch Thomas, about A.D. 848, assisted by Bokam, a wealthy Egyptian, during the reign of el Mamûn, while the Moslems had temporarily abandoned the Holy City on account of a scarcity of food, caused by armies of devastating locusts. The Moslems on their return were astonished and chagrined to find that the Christian Church had arisen from its ruins with so much splendour that it quite diminished the grandeur of the Dome of the Rock, recently restored by el Mamûn, A.D. 831, in the Haram area, on so much lower a level. They therefore took their revenge by imprisoning the patriarch on the charge of having raised his church above that of the Moslems, an accusation so evidently truthful that the patriarch had no prospect of refuting it, until a Moslem, who had an interest in the matter, advised the patriarch simply to deny the fact, and leave the onus of proof upon his accusers. They who would have been ready enough to bolster up any false accusation, were quite unable to prove or substantiate a truth evident to the senses; the patriarch therefore regained his liberty.

Towards the close of the ninth century, Mecca was pillaged by the fanatical Carmathians, the Kaaba was deserted, and the Sakhra, under the Dome of the Rock at Jerusalem, was again for a brief period the Kibleh of the Moslems.

This was an unfortunate turn of affairs for the Christians, for the great influx of Moslem pilgrims to Jerusalem greatly increased the fanaticism and intolerance of those living on the spot, until it culminated, A.D. 937, in a further pillage of the Churches of the Resurrection and Calvary, and in the destruction of the basilica of Constantine.

A few years later the regents of the Grecian Empire endeavoured to regain Syria from the Saracens, and from A.D. 963 to 975, they gained a succession of victories, at one time even threatening Bagdad itself. The Greeks, however, returned without leaving any garrison in Syria, and on their departure a bloody persecution of the Christians commenced, during which the Church of the Holy Sepulchre was again destroyed, and the Patriarch John burnt alive.

A.D. 969, Mucz, the Fatimite, transferred the capital of the Kaliphate from Bagdad to Cairo on the Nile, and was succeeded there by the mad El Hakim of infamous memory: a monster who, after committing numberless atrocities and extravagances, gave himself out to be the Deity Incarnate. In the height of a frenzy, A.D. 1010, and in reply to a complaint from the Moslems, he gave the order for the destruction of the Church of the Resurrection at Jerusalem, which was immediately put into execution, and carried out in its integrity. The walls were razed to the ground by the governor, who even made an attempt to remove the rocky tomb itself, but this intention he did not carry out, and possibly he only threatened it in order to secure a bribe. It is said that the misconduct of the Christians, at Easter-time, at the descent of the Holy Fire gave the Moslems a handle for preferring a complaint against them to El Hakim.

Thus was the second great destruction of the churches of the holy places accomplished.

Temporary buildings were now erected for the accommodation of the enormous number of pilgrims who at this time commenced to flock to the Holy City, during the eleventh century, at a time when the end of the world was yearly expected.

The restoration was eventually taken in hand by the Patriarch Nicephorus, who completed it A.D. 1048, at an enormous expense, principally borne by the Emperor Constantine Monomachus. This restoration consisted of a round church over the Holy Sepulchre, surmounted by a dome, chapels over Golgotha, and other sacred sites, and is described by Sæwulf, A.D. 1103. The whole was afterwards united into one building, as it stands at present, by the Crusaders, A.D. 1120.

The state of the Christians in the eleventh century, at Jerusalem, had become more and more degraded, the clergy and laity alike having sunk to the lowest depths of immorality at the time when crowds of pilgrims began to flock to Jerusalem to pay their devotions at the sacred shrines. While matters were in this state a French hermit, named Peter, a man of unflagging energy and overflowing eloquence, was stirred up in spirit by what he saw around him, and conceived the idea of preaching a crusade (the first). He struck at the right moment, all Europe was upheaved in consequence, and the Crusades were initiated, which, for two centuries, swore to keep alive religious enthusiasm in Europe.

Jerusalem was taken by the Crusaders A.D. 1099.

Hitherto, the difficulties of the Christians regarding the Holy Sepulchre had mainly resulted from the intolerance of the Moslems or the ill-will of the Jews; but now, in addition, a never-ceasing element of internal strife was introduced: for the churches now came to be used by the Christians of both the Latin and Greek rites, and owing to the aggressions of the Latins so much vindictive spirit arose on both sides that it is even related that Jerusalem was eventually betrayed into the hands of the Saracens by the Greek native Christians, who found their yoke less heavy than that of their fellow-Christians of the Latin rite.

The Holy Sepulchre had come under the care of Godfrey, the first Frank King of Jerusalem, renowned among the Crusaders for his purity of morals and pride of arms, but it only experienced for a few months the effect of his power of organisation and the example of his rectitude of conduct. He died, and was succeeded by his brother, Baldwin I., a brave but licentious man; and now Christianity under Christian rule at Jerusalem rapidly became more and more degraded, until all self-respect seemed lost, and the degenerate behaviour of the followers of the Cross cannot bear contrast with the chivalrous actions of the adherents of the Crescent.

Baldwin commenced his reign by quarrelling with the corrupt Patriarch Dagobert, and owing to the machinations of the latter the miracle of the descent of the Holy Fire at Easter-time, A.D. 1100, failed.

The people, astonished and alarmed, for three days made intercession at the sacred shrine, by which time a reconciliation having taken place between the patriarch and the king, the fire suddenly filled the church with a brilliant light, during a solemn procession which was being made barefoot by the king, priests and people. This miraculous interposition served to arouse the flagging religious enthusiasm of the people.

It is somewhat singular that the miracle play of the descent of the Holy Fire at Easter-time has survived the middle ages, and is carried on from year to year to the present day; obviously it is kept up as a political measure, in order that the religious enthusiasm of a great nation (Russia) may be preserved, thus drawing thousands of pilgrims yearly to Jerusalem, causing the necessity for vast Russian buildings and establishments in the Holy Land, which in time of war would be found most useful.

During the occupation of Jerusalem by the Franks, the Knights Templars were organised and the Hospitallers became a military order; the former occupied the buildings of Abd el Melek and Mamûn in the Haram area, while the latter built their Hospice without and adjoining the Holy Sepulchre to the south, on what is called the Muristan.

These two orders, by special permission from the

THE TOMB. 73

pope, were exempt from all episcopal jurisdiction, and subject only to him. The heads of these orders, together with the patriarch, appear to have divided the supreme authority, under the Kings of Jerusalem, and to have been continually quarrelling.

The Knights Hospitallers especially were on the worst of terms with the neighbouring authorities at the Holy Sepulchre, and even descended to such petty means of annoyance as ringing all the bells at the Hospice when the patriarch was proceeding to church, in order to disturb his devotions. They also gave a safe asylum and the last rites of the Church to such as had been excommunicated by the regular clergy, and, in fact, by their behaviour generally, did their utmost to degrade Christianity.

If there had been any doubt, or secret, as to the true site of the Holy Sepulchre known to these contending parties, it is impossible that it could have remained concealed.

In the twelfth century Jerusalem again reverted to the Moslems, under Saladin, and the native Christians enjoyed a religious toleration which they had lacked under the Franks : but they could not forget the infamous manner in which they had been treated ; and the continuance of the division between the Eastern and Western Christians is supposed to be due, in a greater measure, to the ill feeling engendered by the aggressive conduct of the Western Christians during the Frank occupation, than to the pretensions of the Roman pope or doctrinal differences.

In the early portion of the fourteenth century (A.D. 1322) the Church of the Holy Sepulchre was visited by Sir John Maundeville, at which time the sepulchre itself was walled round by the Sultan, because the pilgrims were in the habit of breaking away and carrying off portions of the rock.

About A.D. 1685 the French king requested the Grand Vizier to order the Holy Sepulchre to be put into the hands of the Latins, according to the terms of the capitulations of A.D. 1673. This was carried out in A.D. 1691.

In the seventeenth century (A.D. 1697) the strife between the Greek and Latin communities appears to have come to an issue by the contention on each side for the proprietorship of the Holy Sepulchre. These disputes were carried on with the fury and animosity which characterise such difficulties, causing the traveller, Henry Maundrell, to exclaim with much truth, 'Who can expect ever to see the holy places rescued from the hands of infidels? Or, if they should be recovered, what deplorable contests might be expected to follow them, seeing, even in the present state of captivity, they are made the occasion of such un-Christian rage and animosity.'

A.D. 1808 the Church of the Holy Sepulchre was damaged by fire, and was destroyed to a great extent, with the exception of the sepulchral case itself. The columns which now support the dome are square, but the round columns, much damaged by fire, are still in existence within, with their Latin inscriptions. One of these was seen in 1867, during repairs to the church, by the Austrian Consul.

Up to the year 1867 there was an opening in the dome to the sky overhead above the sepulchre; but on the rebuilding of the dome, 1867-68, this space was all covered in.

PART III.

THE TEMPLE.

In many modern atlases and instructional books we are now accustomed to find the tabernacle represented as a modern European tent, of the description called marquee, such as is often seen at a flower-show in this country.

This idea was first propounded and brought forward about twenty years ago by Mr. Fergusson, and it has been somewhat rapidly taken up by the public, though I do not think that such a representation to the eye of an Arab or Jew (brought up in the East) would call up any idea save that of the travelling tent of a rich Frank tourist.

The oblong box-like structure shown in the works of Calmet, Bähr and Milman is in all probability the real representation of the tabernacle as it existed, for it corresponds to the description given of it in the Bible ; Mr. Fergusson, however, attempts to throw ridicule on this shape (appealing to our English prejudices), by suggesting its likeness to a coffin with a pall thrown over it ; but he does not explain how a likeness to the modern form of coffin should be any objection to its use among a people living three thousand years ago, who used neither coffin nor pall, and whose eyes were then entirely accustomed to buildings of the general shape of our modern coffin.

As a matter of fact, the oblong box (let Mr. Fergusson call it coffin-shaped if he will) was and is the general shape of all the buildings in Egypt and the East generally as far as India: proof of which can be found in the Biblical accounts, in Fergusson's 'History of Architecture,' and in modern photographs; and Mr. Fergusson will find it difficult to produce a specimen of any early building from those countries, dating before our era, with a high-pitched roof similar to that which he proposes for the tabernacle.

It may be said that the tabernacle was only a tent, but I contend that it was not a tent in our sense of the word. It was a wooden box-like building, with a leathern roof—in fact a wooden portable temple.

Admitting however, for the sake of argument, that it was a tent, I ask why it is necessary to give it a high-pitched roof, when Arab tents at the present day are nothing like a marquee. I have passed nights in Bedouin tents, during heavy rains, whose roofs, of one thickness of camels' hair, had a slope of not more than one in six, and they were comparatively dry inside; and I do not see any reason for supposing that the roof of the tabernacle was necessarily, for the sake of dryness, more than a foot higher at the centre than at the sides. Moreover, Mr. Fergusson is very extravagant with the allowance of rainfall which he allows to the desert, thus very much increasing the apparent difficulty of the subject.

He proposes thirty inches or *more* per annum for the desert, which is an amount far in excess of the average fall in many parts of England. I have to suggest that the rainfall in Palestine does not exceed twenty-four inches, and that in the rainless portions of the desert it does not exceed six to eight inches per annum.

He further suggests that, with the box-like structure, the roof would have sagged in; but in his construction he is obliged to introduce ridge-poles and uprights which are not mentioned in the Bible, with the use of half of which the box-shaped tabernacle would have its roof so held up as not to sag to any inconvenient extent. And further, in order to maintain his theory, he is obliged to do 'considerable violence to the text' of the Bible, and assumes the existence of errors in it, which he ventures to rectify. (*Vide* 'The Temples of the Jews,' p. 22.)

He introduces a very grave difficulty by using a high-pitched roof, for it would have been open throughout from east to west, and the wind would have easily raised the roof, and have blown it off with facility. Again, he leaves the Holy of Holies without any ceiling, except the angular roof of the tent: it thus ceases to be a *cube*, and is open to the *light* and air to the west, so that any person on an elevation to west could *see* into it. Such a construction is entirely contrary to the Biblical account, in which the entire seclusion of the sanctum is dwelt upon, and the interior spoken of as 'thick darkness.'

He also points out that in the box-shaped tabernacle, the ornamental curtain would only have been partially seen, whereas in his hypothetical form most of it would have been seen. But in this argument he appears to miss the whole object of the tabernacle, and seems to think that its only use was for its interior to delight the eyes of the priests. Rather may we suppose that it mattered little how much of the ornamental curtain was seen by mortal eye. If the choice work of the tabernacle had been intended for view, the embroidered curtain might have been used as a covering outside instead of the rough badger-skins. The whole account goes to show that the box was for the enshrinement of the most precious jewel any nation could possess; and, therefore, with a rough covering on the outside, the hangings and furniture of the structure were made more and more costly the closer they were to the jewel they were intended to enshroud. There is nothing inconsistent in the covering of the golden-laden boards with an embroidered cloth, and that again with goats' hair. The precious Shekinah might well be carefully housed.

Those who wish to study the subject can judge for themselves how closely Calmet's box-shaped tabernacle corresponds in its dimensions with those given in the Bible: I only desire here to show the very great objections to Mr. Fergusson's hypothetical form—a form which is inimical to the statement that the tabernacle was reproduced in stone with all its proportions doubled. It is evident that if there had been any such form of roof to the tabernacle, we should have some trace of it in the form of the Temple, or in the architecture of the country, whereas we only find references made to flat roofs, and only find flat roofs still existing. It is quite impossible to suppose that the Temple was in the form of a very large marquee tent, and yet this is the conclusion to which Mr. Fergusson would force us. He evidently is now aware of the great difficulty he has introduced for his theory, as in 'The Temples of the Jews' he attempts to construct the transverse section of the Temple upon a triangle—an equilateral triangle—for he is now obliged to discard the right-angled triangle on which he constructed the tabernacle.

Curiously enough, he further suggests (in a somewhat unorthodox strain) that this very modern-looking marquee-shaped tabernacle had its origin from some sacred tent of the Arabs of Midian, or some neighbouring tribe, thus bringing in a very strong argument against his own theory, for there is *another* tabernacle, the Kaaba at Mecca, and it is described as an oblong box-like structure, and if less ancient than the tabernacle, was possibly copied from it.

THE TEMPLE OF HEROD.

I have already in the first part ('Parallel Holiness of Mounts Zion and Moriah') shown that the threshing-

THE TEMPLE OF HEROD.

THE TEMPLE. 81

floor of Araunah the Jebusite was situated on the eastern hill of Jerusalem, called Mount Moriah, on which now stands the ancient wall of the Noble Sanctuary, which all authorities agree in attributing to either Herod or Solomon. All writers also agree in declaring that the Temple was situated somewhere within the space enclosed by the walls of the Noble Sanctuary, though they differ as to its position and as to the extent of its court.

In the first place let us denude the hill of its present covering and walls, and look at it as it originally stood. For this purpose I give a contoured plan of the rock on Mount Moriah, which I made in 1869-70, somewhat similar to one on which Lieutenant Conder subsequently constructed a contoured plan in 1875.

Now these two plans, so far as the disputed portions are concerned, agree very closely as to the position of the contours, and I shall give that as sufficient reply to Mr. Fergusson's proposition that there is a precipice of rock at the south-west angle, on which he now would place his hypothetical temple. I say, and I think surveyors generally will bear me out, that with our present knowledge of the levels, the line of contours as given by me cannot be altered in the manner Mr. Fergusson would propose.

Now it will be observed that Moriah is a hill between two valleys, about 900 feet across. The ridge of Moriah runs from north-west to south-east, the western valley running parallel to the ridge, while the eastern valley runs nearly north and south. The ridge slopes from north-west to south-east, falling within the length of the sanctuary walls, from 2,450 to 2,380, or 70 feet.

On the north there is another wide valley, running into that on the east, thus still further curtailing the limits of the hill, so that the summit may be said to be a narrow plateau bounded by contour 2,420, about 600 feet from north to south, and about 500 feet wide on the north, and 150 wide to the south. It is obvious that the threshing-floor must have stood somewhere in this area, because they are always flat surfaces, and could not possibly be placed on the steep sloping sides of a rocky mountain.

The sides of this mount are very steep on the south-west side. Where Mr. Fergusson would place his hypothetical temple the slope is so steep that it would be impracticable to attempt to climb up without using hands as well as feet, the rise in one place being 60 feet in 100 feet horizontal; and again, 110 feet in 250 feet horizontal.

It is to be observed that the south-west angle of the Noble Sanctuary reaches right across the Tyropœon valley, and ascends 30 feet of the hill on the opposite side; it is self-evident that this could not have been the original position of the Temple, but is an extension. The south-east angle also rests upon a point on the hill-side, down in the Cedron valley, 170 feet below the level of the Sacred Rock.

The north-east angle likewise crosses over a valley at a level 2,290, or 150 feet below the level of the

Sacred Rock; and the north-west angle runs up the rising hill of Bezetha. No unprejudiced person can look upon the contoured plan of the Rock of Mount Moriah, and read the descriptions of the positions of the altar, without feeling convinced that the Temple was placed somewhere on the raised platform surrounding the Dome of the Rock.

The references to the building of the Temple on the high part of the mountain are very numerous. Ezekiel xliii. 12 : 'This is the law of the house. Upon the top of the mountain the whole limit thereof round about shall be most holy.'

The Talmud always terms it the *mountain of the house*, and describes the courts rising one above another until the highest platform is reached, namely, that of the Holy of Holies. And as they assert that there was rock exposed in the Holy of Holies, they must have supposed that this was the highest point of the mountain.

Dr. Chaplin, in summing up the Talmudic evidence, states: 'The teaching of the Talmudic doctors therefore indicates clearly that the *aven shetiyeh* was rock, and not a detached stone, projecting three finger-breadths from the floor of the Holy of Holies, covering a cavity which was regarded as the mouth of an abyss, reverenced as the centre and foundation of the world, and having the ineffable name of God inscribed on it.'

This evidently appears to apply to the Sacred Rock under the Dome, and it is clear that the Moslems have taken their traditions regarding their Sacred Rock from the Talmudists.

This is very much in favour of the Sacred Rock itself being the Holy of Holies, and I am not positive that the position I assign it (a few feet south of the rock) is the absolute position ; I only assert that in the position where I place it, it fulfils the conditions required most thoroughly, and that Mr. Fergusson is altogether in error in his disposition.

Josephus is most positive in his statements. *Ant.*, viii. 3, § 9 : 'When Solomon had filled up great valleys with earth, and had elevated the ground [for] four hundred cubits, he made it to be on a level with the *top of the mountain on* which the Temple was built.'

Bel., v. 5, § 1 : 'Now this temple was built upon a stony hill. At first the *plain at the top* was hardly sufficient for *the holy house and the altar.*'

These accounts seem only applicable to the location of the Temple on the platform of the Dome of the Rock.

One of the first questions that arises is that regarding the extent occupied by Herod's Temple enclosure, and upon this subject there has been much bitter antagonism among the several authorities ; some giving it as but 600 feet per side, others taking the whole Noble Sanctuary, others taking but a portion of this area. It is to be noted that Mr. Fergusson is compelled to limit his temple to 600 feet per side, in order to have room for his hypothetical Holy Sepulchre at the Dome of the Rock.

THE TEMPLE.

Let us see now what dimensions are given by the various ancient authorities.

No information is given concerning the extent of Solomon's Temple area in the Bible; all we have there is that his palace was near the Temple.

In the Book of Ezekiel we are able to glean some information, but how to make use of it is a question not yet settled. Mr. Fergusson in his restoration makes six courts of a hundred cubits each, while Dr. Currey, in 'The Speaker's Commentary of the Bible,' gives a much larger area. I have not been able as yet to arrive at any deductions from the vision of the seer that will throw light upon the subject we have in hand.

Our next authority is the Talmud, which makes the Mountain of the House 500 cubits square.

This, according to Mr. Fergusson, would give 750 feet, with a cubit of 18 inches. With a cubit of 21 inches it would give 875 feet.

Our third and last authority is Josephus.

His testimony, so far as descriptions are concerned, is always valuable, but his figures contradict each other very much.

For example, he states most explicitly and circumstantially that the porch of Solomon was 400 cubits in length, and that the Temple-court of Solomon was 400 cubits a side. He then tells us that Herod doubled the area of Solomon's Temple, but that it was still a square. This would give a side of about 565 cubits, equal to 988 feet,

Now the width of the Noble Sanctuary at the southern end is 922 feet, and at the Golden Gate 997 feet.

Again, he tells us that the Temple enclosure with the Antonia was six stadia in circuit, and taking an average of 950 feet for the width of the Noble Sanctuary, this would include the whole of the sanctuary for 1,355 feet from the south wall.

In another passage, however, Josephus would appear to say that the Temple of Herod itself was only a stadium per side—that is 600 feet.

I give, however, the various passages:

Ant., viii. 3, § 9.—'For when he [Solomon] had filled up great valleys with earth, which, on account of their immense depth, could not be looked on when you bended down to see them, without pain, and had elevated the ground [for] *four hundred cubits*, he made it on a level with the top of the mountain on which the Temple was built, and by this means the outmost temple, which was exposed to the air, was even with the Temple itself.'

Ant., xv. 11, § 3.—'This hill it was which Solomon, who was the first of our kings, by divine revelation, encompassed with a wall. . . . . This hill was walled all round, and in compass *four stadia*, each angle containing in length a stadium.'

Ant., xv. 11, § 5.—'The length was a stadium,' referring to the Stoa Basilica of Herod.

Ant., xx. 9, § 7.—'These cloisters belonged to the outer court, and were situated in a deep valley, and *had walls that reached* 400 *cubits* [in length], and were built of square and very white stones, the length of each of which stones was twenty cubits, and their height six cubits. *This was the work of King Solomon.*

Ant., xv. 11, § 1.—'*Herod*, in the eighteenth year of his reign, and after the acts already mentioned, undertook a very great work, that is, to build of himself the Temple of God, and to make it *larger in compass.*'

Bel., i. 21, § 1.—' Accordingly in the fifteenth year of his reign, *Herod* rebuilt the Temple, and encompassed a piece of land about it with a wall ; *which land was twice as large as that before enclosed.*'

Bel., v. 5, § 2.—'The cloisters were in breadth thirty cubits, while the entire compass of it was, by measure, *six stadia, including the Antonia.*'

Bel., vi. 5, § 4.—' For the Jews, by demolishing the Antonia, had made their Temple four-square, while at the same time they had written in their sacred oracle " that then should the city be taken, as well as their Holy House, when once their Temple had become four-square." '

From the above it will be seen that there are great discrepancies in the accounts of Josephus. He tells us that the old cloisters of King Solomon were 400 cubits in length ; that Herod, in rebuilding the Temple, encompassed a piece of ground twice as large as that before enclosed, and yet that the Stoa Basilica of Herod measured only a stadium or 600 feet, and that the Temple enclosure of Herod, including the Antonia, measured six stadia.

There is evidently at least one error in this account, if it is not totally in error, so far as figures are concerned. I assume that Josephus did not accurately know the dimensions of the Temple, and was speaking at a venture.

Before we proceed further it will be desirable to inquire into the relative positions of the various portions of the Noble Sanctuary, and refer them, if practicable, to surrounding walls or to any central object.

Viewing the plan of the Noble Sanctuary with this object, we are at once struck with the manner in which the lines are disposed.

1. There are cuttings across the general direction of the crest of the hill, as for example the great ditch north of the platform of the Dome of the Rock. This is probably the oldest feature we are able at present to distinguish on the Temple platform.

2. There are walls and buildings perpendicular or parallel to, and therefore referable to, the great east wall.

3. There are the walls and buildings severally perpendicular to, or parallel to, the west and south walls.

Under No. 2 come the following: *a.* The northern wall of the sanctuary; *b.* The scarped rock of Antonia; *c.* The northern edge of the Dome of the Rock platform; *d.* The western side of the Sacred Rock itself; *e.* The Golden Gate.

Under No. 3 are ranged the Jamia al Aksah, the Dome of the Rock, the south side of the Dome of the Rock platform.

It will thus be seen that the Dome of the Rock can be referred to the same origin of building as the Aksah, viz. the west and south sides, while the cutting in the Sacred Rock itself can be referred to the Golden Gate and eastern side; so evident is this, that the singular alteration in the position of the existing Dome of the Rock, made by Mr. Fergusson (in plate vii., 'The Temples of the Jews'), is at once apparent, though how he can alter the position of a building which still exists, is not understood.

If this question is worked out, it will appear obvious that the long cutting on the Rock of the Dome was anterior to the building of the Dome, and, therefore, must have existed when the Dome was built. This is one of the 'damning evidences' against Mr. Fergusson's theory, for it prevents his asserting that the Dome of the Rock was too far from the Golden Gate and north side of the platform to require its being built carefully with reference to their lines.

Having thus seen that existing remains may be divided into groups, let us further examine the ground in detail for any indications which may enable us to fix precisely the limits of Herod's Temple. Here we at once meet with success. We ascertain that the northern limit of the Temple enclosure is now to be seen in the northern end of the Dome of the Rock platform, and that the south, east, and west sides are still in existence, and represented by the south, east, and west sides of the Noble Sanctuary. And at the same time we can fix the site of the Temple itself to within a few feet. We may say for certain that the Holy of Holies and altar were somewhere on the Dome of the Rock platform, between the southern end and an east and west line passing through the Sacred Rock, for the following reasons :

It is stated that King Agrippa built himself a dining-room, overlooking the inner court of the Temple, in the palace of the Asmoneans, which was situated at the northern extremity of the Upper City overlooking the Xystus, where the bridge (Bab as Silsile) joined the Temple to the Xystus.

The passages in Josephus are as follows :

Ant., xv. 11, § 5.—' Now in the western quarter of the enclosure of the Temple there were four gates ; the first led to the *king's palace*, and went to a passage over the intermediate valley.'

Bel., ii. 16, § 3.—' He therefore called the multitude together into the Xystus, and placed his sister Bernice in the house of the Asmoneans, that she might be seen by them—which house was over the Xystus, at the *extremity* of the Upper City, where the bridge joined the Temple to the Xystus.'

Ant., xx. 8, § 11.—' About the same time King Agrippa built himself a very large dining-room in the *royal palace* at Jerusalem, near to the Xystus. Now this palace had been erected of old by the children of Asmoneus, and was situated upon an elevation, and afforded a most delightful prospect to those that had a mind to take a view of the city, which prospect was desired by the king ; and there he could lie down and eat, and thence observe what was done in the Temple, which thing when the chief men of Jerusalem saw they were very much displeased at it. . . . . They therefore erected a wall upon the uppermost building which belonged to the inner court of the Temple, towards the west ; which wall, when it was built, did not only intercept the prospect of the dining-room in the palace, but also of the western cloister that belonged to the outer court of the Temple also, where it was that the Romans kept guard for the Temple at the festivals."

Now the site of this dining-room can be fixed to a few feet, as we know where the extremity of the Upper City is, both to north and to east, and it is described as being at the north-east angle, adjoining the bridge (which still exists), and overlooking the Xystus. And as all agree that the Temple and courts lay generally east and west, it follows that any person looking over from the west, could only see down into the courts in an east and west direction. Therefore it is evident that King Agrippa in looking down from his palace must have looked nearly due east, either along the inner court south of the Temple or north of it. Now the line he must have looked along nearly coincides with the southern side of the Dome of the Rock platform, and therefore we have the certainty that this southern side marks either the northern or southern space between the Temple and its inner court ; that is to say, we have only two positions for the Temple to have been placed in, so far as its latitude is concerned. This in itself completely overthrows Mr. Fergusson's argument regarding the site of the Temple, as where he places it King Agrippa could not have seen what was going on in the Temple courts.

I will now point out the considerations which show that it was into the inner court, south of the Temple, that King Agrippa looked, and thus shall obtain directly a position for the Temple.

I have already shown that Zion, or Akra, occupied the Lower City, to the south-east of the site of the present Holy Sepulchre, and immediately north of the palace of Agrippa, separated from it by the Tyropœon valley. This Akra was about three hundred feet west of the sanctuary wall, in a line drawn between the Dome of the Rock and the northern edge of the platform.

Now we are told, *Ant.*, xii. 9, § 3 : 'At this time it was that the garrison in the Akra at Jerusalem, with the Jewish runagates, did a great deal of harm to the Jews ; for the soldiers that were in that garrison rushed out upon the sudden, and destroyed such as were going up to the Temple in order to offer sacrifices, for this Akra adjoined to and overlooked the Temple.'

And this account will only admit of the Temple courts lying close under, that is due east of, the Akra. This at once fixes the site of the Temple and its courts, showing that it was down the space to the south side of the Temple that King Agrippa could look from his palace.

Having thus fixed the position of the Temple to within a few feet, I will now proceed to give some of the reasons why the exterior walls were as already indicated.

It is stated by Josephus, *Ant.*, xiv. 4, § 2: 'Pompey pitched his tent within [the walls of Jerusalem] on the north part of the Temple, where it was more practicable ; but even on that side there were great towns, and a ditch had been dug, and a deep valley begirt it round about.'

Bel., i. 7, § 3.—' But Pompey himself filled up the ditch that was on the north side of the Temple, and the entire valley also.'

Now from the south side of the sanctuary along the ridge of Mount Moriah, there is the continuous rock, without cut, ditch, or valley, as far as the northern edge of the Dome of the Rock platform. So that this fact alone is sufficient to overthrow Mr. Fergusson's theory, as he has no ditch to the north of his hypothetical temple's site. But on the northern side of the Dome of the Rock platform I found the rock cut in the form of a precipice, and the ridge is there cut in two ; moreover, there is a deep valley to north-east as far as the Pool of Bethesda (Birket Israel), thus exactly corresponding to the above account of Josephus. And further, in this cut rock I discovered the Gate Tadi which was situated in the north wall of the Temple outer court. Thus we have the certainty that this northern side of the Dome of the Rock platform represents the north wall of the Temple courts as it existed in the time of Pompey, and the presumption that it was so in the time of Herod : presumption I say, because I think it is still a question how far the north-eastern portion was occupied by the Temple courts in the time of Herod. Now we know that along the outer walls of the Temple were cloisters (*Bel.*, v. 5, § 2), and it will be seen that the Golden Gate (the old foundations of which are still *in situ*) formed a continuation of the double wall of the northern cloisters to the east, just as the arch (discovered by Dr. Robinson) led from the southern cloisters to the west. The Talmud says, 'Upon the east gate was portrayed the city Shushan. Through it one could see the high-priest who burnt the heifer, and all his assistants going out to the Mount of Olives.' There appear to have been steps or arches leading down from this gate into the Cedron towards the east, and leading up again past the southern end of the site of the present Garden of Gethsemane. Even now (*vide* Ordnance Survey Plan $\frac{1}{10000}$) there are stone walls in the valley which perhaps may indicate the position of those steps, and where remains of them may yet be found. They appear to have ascended again to the east, and reaching the present road to Bethany, to have continued south-east to a level spot at 2,460 feet, just below some existing ruins shown on the Survey plans, where tradition places the site of the altar for the sin offering. From these ruins, if a line is drawn perpendicular to the east wall of the sanctuary, it will cut somewhat to south of the Dome of the Rock. And, therefore, from this spot a view could have been obtained direct over the east wall, through the Gate Nicanor, over the altar into the sanctuary. The production of this visual

THE TEMPLE COURTS.

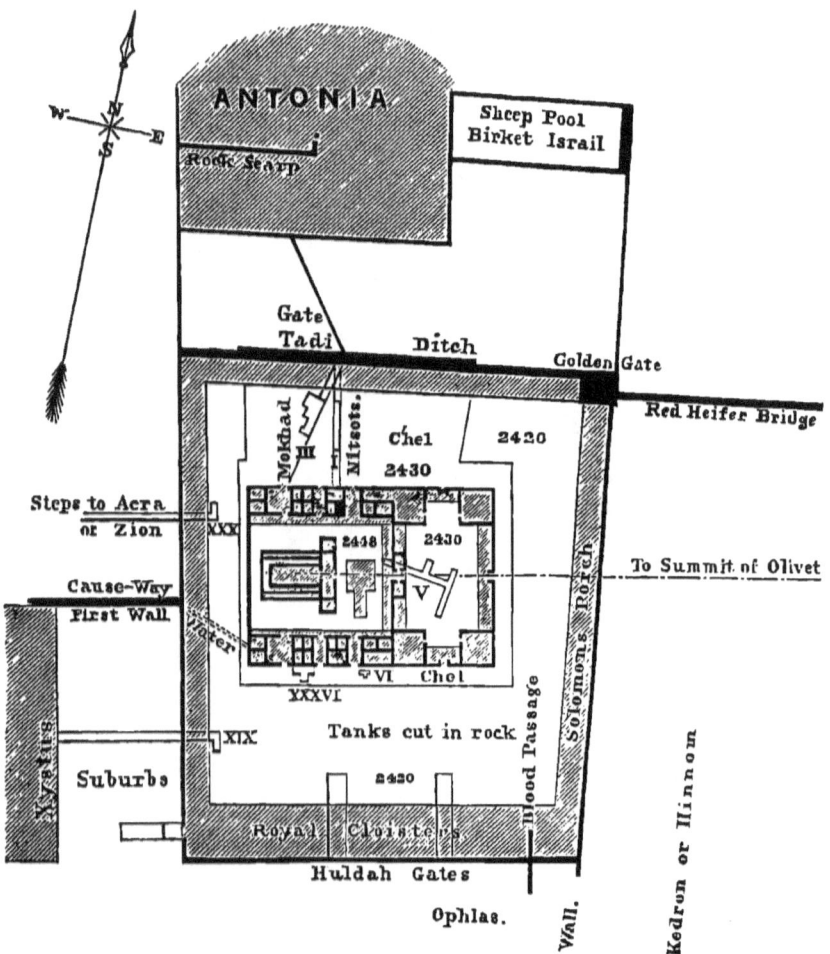

line to the east passes through the centre of the present open court of the Ascension on the summit of Olivet. The Talmud says, 'And all the walls there were high, except the eastern wall, that the priest who burned the heifer might stand on the top of the Mount of Olives, and look straight into the door of the sanctuary when he sprinkled the blood.'

It is thus apparent that it was over the eastern wall, not through the east gate, that the priest on the Mount of Olives looked towards the altar, in front of the Temple.

We thus find so far that this eastern wall with its Golden Gate corresponds to the old wall, and if we pursue the subject still further, the coincidences render the matter a certainty. This wall is built up from the valley, from a height of 2,277 feet above the Mediterranean, until it reaches the level of the Noble Sanctuary at 2,420 feet. It is thus 143 feet in height; and if about sixty feet be added for the cloisters, we have a height of 200 feet. The valley itself at bottom is 2,170 feet, thus we have a height of 300 feet from the bottom of the valley to the top of the cloisters. No wonder then that Josephus said, 'For while the valley was very deep, and its bottom could not be seen, if you looked from above into the depth, this further vastly high elevation of the cloister stood upon that height, insomuch that if anyone looked down from the top of the battlements, or down both those altitudes, he would be giddy, while his sight could not reach to such an immense depth.'

This description could not possibly apply to the hypothetical site which Mr. Fergusson gives the east wall of the Temple, viz., on the blank ridge of the rock. We have, moreover, found on the walls at great depths (from 80 to 100 feet) old Phœnician marks cut and painted on the stones, so that even Mr. Fergusson is obliged to allow that this wall dates from the time of Solomon, and agrees with me that at the south-east angle it forms part of Solomon's Temple, though by his theory concerning the sepulchre, he is obliged to stop here, and cannot take up my view that King Herod brought Solomon's palace into the sanctuary, and made it a portion of the Temple area.

If we take now the southern side of the Noble Sanctuary, we will again see that it fully agrees with the description given of it in the Talmud and in Josephus.

Its angles to the east and west are built up from the depths of the adjoining valleys, so that if a man looked 'down both those altitudes, he would be giddy.' No other position would suit the various references to the wall. The Talmud says, 'Two Huldah gates in the south, which served for going in and going out;' and accordingly we find the double and triple (formerly a double gate) still existing.

In the same manner we find the west wall corresponds with the description of Josephus and the Talmud, though it should be remarked that the latter mentions but one gate, while the former mentions four.

Ant., xv. 11, § 5.—' Now in the western quarter of the enclosures of the Temple there were four gates; the first led to the king's palace, and went to a passage over the intermediate valley.' This is the Bab as Silsile, which leads over the great causeway to the palace of the Asmoneans at the north-east extremity of the Upper City.

' Two more led to the suburbs of the city.' These are the two southern gates in the west wall at Robinson's Arch, and Bab al Magharibe.

' And the last led to the other city, where the road descended down into the valley by a great number of steps, and thence up again by the ascent.' This is the gate I discovered leading to Akra from the Bab al Mathara.

The reasons generally why the present exterior walls of the Noble Sanctuary, so far north as the Golden Gate, should be coincident with the outer walls of Herod's Temple enclosure are most numerous. All local indications favour this supposition, and I know of no reason yet given for the Temple enclosure being of less area than this, excepting the statement of Josephus that the fourth cloister was a stadium in length; and as he contradicts this in several other passages, there is actually no standing ground for Mr. Fergusson's theory that the Temple was only a stadium on each side. The fact is, as already frequently pointed out, Josephus can be relied upon for his descriptions, but he evidently had a very bad memory for figures. Even Mr. Fergusson, while insisting that this great error of Josephus must be accepted, is obliged frequently to alter his other figures to suit his own measurements, and has to propose that he means feet when he says cubits. But then, however, it is not the text of Josephus only that Mr. Fergusson alters, for he acknowledges that in order to support his argument he has to do 'considerable violence to the text' of the Book of Exodus, he wants to show that the text of the Book of Ezekiel is wrong, and accuses the Book of Chronicles of exaggeration. Until, therefore, Mr. Fergusson can show some cause why the Temple area should have been less than I have indicated, I see little use in passing in review the several other proofs I have given in other works ('Recovery of Jerusalem,' 'Underground Jerusalem,' 'Palestine Quarterly Statements') that the Temple area is indicated by the present sanctuary walls south of the Golden Gate. To show how completely the present plan of the Noble Sanctuary corresponds with the description of the early writers, I may mention that in 1869 I took the plan constructed by the Rev. John Lightfoot, D.D., in the year 1664, made (from his own statement) entirely from the ancient writings, his mind being unbiassed by any knowledge of the present Noble Sanctuary, and drew it to scale, making the southern wall coincide with the southern wall of the Noble Sanctuary. When this was done it was a plan of Herod's enclosure, occupying the southern portion of the Noble Sanctuary, being nearly a square of about 950 feet, with a compass of about six furlongs.

Comparing this plan with the ground, I found that the two Huldah gates of Dr. Lightfoot rest upon the double and triple gates of the south sanctuary wall. His causeway, and two of his gates, are represented by Wilson's Arch, Barclay's Gate, and Robinson's Arch, except that he pushes each of these about fifty feet too far to the north. His fourth gate falls south of (Bab as Silsile) his causeway, and it is not represented by any gateway that we have been able to find. But there is north of Bab as Silsile, and near Bab al Mathara, a tunnel through the sanctuary wall, corresponding in some respects with Barclay's Gateway, which I suppose to be the fourth gate leading to the other city, or Akra, by a great number of steps down into the city, and thence up again by the ascent. This may be the Gate *Kipunus* spoken of in the Mishna, the meaning of which word is 'hole,' or 'through passage' (*vide* 'Prospect of Jerusalem,' p. 226), giving a correct description of this vaulted descent.

To the north he places Tadi, in the centre of the length of the wall; but we find a rock-cut passage closely corresponding to Tadi, not in the centre of the wall, but at the same distance from the west cloisters as is his West Huldah Gate (double gate) in the south wall.

With regard to the Temple itself, we find that his southern and eastern sides nearly coincide with the south and east walls of the Dome of the Rock platform, and that the altar stands over a curious rock-cut passage that now is used as a tank, and which is evidently a tunnel blocked up.

We have thus, between Dr. Lightfoot's plan and the present plan of the Noble Sanctuary, a number of points of resemblance which show that the identification of the position of the Temple is not such a mere haphazard arrangement on my part as Mr. Fergusson wishes to induce the public to imagine. One of Dr. Lightfoot's remarks is specially worthy of mention, as he made it without any knowledge of the Noble Sanctuary, and before Mr. Fergusson brought out his theory.

He says that in the southern wall 'the gates were so set as that there was an equal space between gate and gate, and betwixt gate and the corners of the wall;' and further, 'And so is Josephus to be understood when he saith, " The fourth part of the wall was to the south, and had gates in the middle."'

This is a matter of some moment, as Mr. Fergusson, in spite of the clear statements of the Talmud, puts the two Huldah gates in one at the double gate.

The fact, however, of the wall of Ophal joining the southern wall at the south-east angle, is really in itself certain proof that the southern cloister extended to the south-east angle, and is a complete refutation of Mr. Fergusson's statements.

Ant., v. 4, § 3.—'[The old wall] reaches as far as a certain place which they called " Ophlas," where it was joined to the eastern cloister of the Temple.'

I will now proceed to point out the principal local

indication within the Temple walls. And for this purpose I have constructed a plan of the Temple and its courts, principally from the Talmud, assuming a cubit of twenty-one inches, and I lay it upon the plan of the Noble Sanctuary, in such a manner that King Agrippa could have seen into its court from his dining-room window in his palace, and so that the Macedonians in Akra could have dominated it; this position is also in accordance with the Talmud which says, that without the inner court, 'the largest space was on the south, the second on the east, the third on the north, and the least westward.'

Having done this, I find that the position of the Temple is almost identical with that which I obtained by laying Dr. Lightfoot's plan over the plan of the present sanctuary, although I differ in details of courts somewhat, as the size of the chambers can only be obtained from the descriptions, in the absence of measurements.

The altar stands over the western end of the Souterrain No. V., a remarkable underground passage, which may well have served as a communication under the courts of the Temple, in connection with the great water system necessary for keeping clean the Temple courts.

Whether it may have led from the altar to the Blood passage, which I discovered at the south-east angle of the Noble Sanctuary, in the south wall, or whether it connected the gates Mokad and Nitsots with the water works, or whether it was the underground communication to the Gate Nicanor (Ant., xv. 11, § 7) under which it runs is not yet certain ; possibly it may have served for all these purposes, but in either case it would have been a passage of some importance. There is a legend in Mejir ed Din that one of the ancient kings threw a roll from Olivet, which fell near the portion of raised platform where No. V. Souterrain is situated. It is possible that this legend may have some reference to the concealment of the lost volume of the sacred law in this Souterrain.

The three gates to the inner court, both on north and south, are placed at equal intervals from each other, and from the corners of the courts. The Gate Nitsots falls in such a manner that the Sakhra Cave entrance opens into it. This cave would appear to be continued through into Souterrain No. I., forming a passage to the Gate Tadi. This may be the passage into the chel mentioned in the Talmud as leading from Nitsots, and, if in connection with No. V. Souterrain, it would have been the occult passage mentioned by Josephus, Ant., xv. 11, § 7 : 'There was also an occult passage built for the king : it led from Antonia to the inner Temple, at its eastern gate ; over which he also erected for himself a tower, that he might have the opportunity of a subterranean ascent to the Temple, in order to guard against any sedition which might be made by the people against their kings.'

Between the Gate Nitsots and the Gate Corban lies the rock over which the present Dome of the Rock is constructed. On this fall the chambers of the washers and of Parva. The drain I discovered on the top of the rock may be the passage by which the refuse from the 'inwards' were carried off.

The chamber Parva lies directly over the Sakhra Cave, and the notes in the Talmud are sufficiently curious, and appear to establish an identification.

'Parvah is the name of a man who was a magician, and there are some of the wise men that say that he digged a vault under the ground till he could come to see what the high-priest did on the day of expiation.'

The gates, according to the Talmud, were 46¾ cubits from centre to centre, and if we produce the Souterrain No. III. upon the line of the inner court, we find it falls upon the Gate Mokad. The position of this Souterrain and the chambers in it appear to coincide very closely to the chambers spoken of as leading from Mokad. It passes obliquely towards where Souterrain No. I. runs out at the Gate Tadi, on the northern edge of the raised platform of the Dome of the Rock.

We are told that the meaning of *Tadi* is *obscurity*. The Talmud says, 'Tadi served for no [ordinary] purpose ;' and further, 'that it was used by the priests to retire by, should they have become defiled during their service in the Temple.' We read further on, 'All the gates had lintels, except Tadi ; there two stones inclined one upon another.' Then we read again that the Gate Nitsots 'had a door into the chel, and that to the house Mokad were two doors open to the chel.' Again, with regard to the house Mokad, 'in the north-east [chamber] they descended to the House of Baptism.' And again, the priest 'rose and went out in the gallery that ran under the arch, and candles flamed on each side until he came to the House of Baptism.' Rabbi Eleazer, the son of Jacob, says, 'In the gallery that went under the chel he passed out through Tadi.'

Dr. Lightfoot, in his commentaries, says that the priests, after suffering defilement, 'were to bathe as was said before, and the way to the bathing-place is expressed in these words : " He goeth down a turning staircase that went under the Temple." Therefore, it is hard to say which way this passage to the bathing-place lay, since the word will enlarge it to any part of the Temple. It appeareth it was some vault underground, through which they passed ; into which vault they went down by a turning pair of stairs, out of the north-west room of Beth Mokad. And from thence whither they went, whether under the chel, as Rabbi Eleazer conceiveth, or under some part of the court or mountain of the house, it is but in vain to search. It seemeth the bath was underground, and a room by it with a fire in it to warm themselves at when they had done bathing.'

We have then the certainty that the passage from Mokad to the House of Baptism was underground, and the probability that the underground passage to the Gate Tadi was on the same level.

Now we find on the ground that Nitsots is over the

cave of the Sakhra, that Souterrain No. I. is a tunnel leading in the direction of Tadi, and that at Tadi is the precipitous rock bounding the platform to the north, also that there is a passage leading from Tadi to Mokad, corresponding to the description given of it above.

In the southern side of the inner court the chamber of the draw-well lies just north of Cistern No. VI., and not far from No. XXXVI., which two cisterns are in communication with the large tanks of the southern portion of the Noble Sanctuary, and with the water-supply from Solomon's pools and Wady Byar. Dr. Lightfoot supposes the house of Abtinas to have been over the chamber of the draw-well, and the Talmud tells us that the priests guarded the sanctuary in three places. In the house of Abtinas, in the house of Nitsots, and in the house of Mokad. We now see the reason why the priests were selected for this duty at these points, namely, because they were underground communications with the sanctuary which needed to be carefully watched.

Now with regard to the levels of the Temple and its courts, Mr. Fergusson states that where I place the Sakhra it 'would be buried so deep in a mass of masonry it would be utterly obliterated, and be neither ornamental nor useful to anybody.'

I do not comprehend how he can have mistaken my meaning in the face of the levels and account I have given in the 'Recovery of Jerusalem,' from which he frequently quotes; but in order to dispel all doubts on the subject, I will now give the levels.

The level of the Court of the Gentiles was the general level of the present Noble Sanctuary, namely 2,420 feet above the Mediterranean Sea; on this level is also that of the causeway from Bab as Silsile, leading to the Upper City. The level of the Court of the Women was 2,430 feet, and that of the inner court 2,448 feet, the present surface of the Sacred Rock inside the chambers being 2,440 feet; but we have no indication that the chambers were on a level with the inner court, in fact there is a supposition that they were below the inner court. The probabilities are that the top of the Sakhra was nearly on a level with the chamber of Parva but was not visible.

PART IV.

THE TEMPLE OR THE TOMB.—INTRODUCTORY.

THE study of the works of Mr. Fergusson on the holy site, so far as the light they throw upon the topography of the Holy City is concerned, would scarcely repay the labour to be spent on them, owing to the numberless errors in which they abound, were they not valuable works from another point of view.

They afford a rare opportunity for closely observing the mental process by which problems are worked out and conclusions arrived at in the mind of a very talented writer. There can be no doubt that this process differs in individuals according to their nature, and that few of us are conscious of the exact manner in which we arrive at results and form opinions, and that it is seldom that we have a good opportunity of observing this process in others.

Mr. Fergusson, however, is by no means reticent in these matters, and describes to us the exact process by which he suddenly leapt to a conclusion, thirty-five years ago, as to the date of the building of the Dome of the Rock, and how he manages to find in everything, something to support his theory.

His theory in itself, to those who know the sacred places at Jerusalem, who have studied their history, and are aware of the utter impossibility of the location of the Holy Sepulchre on the Sakhra, appears to be that of a person deceived by one of the pious frauds attempted in the middle ages upon the ignorant, rather than the well-weighed reasonings of a talented author.

Yet indeed, on the other hand, I must confess that I never can peruse his works on the subject without a feeling that his theory is 'ludicrously impossible,' and that after all it is but labour lost to refute him. For he may be simply seeing how far the public can be hoaxed; that he may really be aware of the impossibility of his theory, but that having once given his opinions rashly, he intends to hold to them, and enjoys the innocent fooling of the public as a grim jest. As though relying upon his vigour of language, intricacy of argument, reputation, and learning, he may induce the intellects of the public to bow down before him, and accept his unestablished statements.

But as I cannot suppose this to be actually the case, I feel it necessary to accept his propositions as put forward in all sober earnestness, and to point out the very curious errors in which he has enveloped himself. I shall accomplish this by giving no less than forty erroneous statements of his, together with my remarks on the same; but before doing this, I propose to refer generally to his system of argument.

As an example of his process of reasoning, I will

take his article 'Jerusalem' in 'Smith's Biblical Dictionary.' There he wishes to fix the site of the tower of Hippicus at the present north-west corner of the modern city (where Psephinus is usually placed), thus bringing the present Holy Sepulchre within his hypothetical first wall, and by this act disestablishing its authenticity, as the Holy Sepulchre was without the first and second walls. His process is as follows: Contrary to all traditions and all local indications, he assumes that the first wall was continued beyond the traditional tower of Hippicus in the citadel, to north along the present wall of city up to north-west angle, where Psephinus is usually located, thus placing the traditional Hippicus in a re-entering angle, and then says of it: 'In the first place he (Josephus) made it a corner tower, whereas at the time he wrote, the tower in the citadel must have been in a re-entering angle as it is now.' That is to say, he first alters all the topography to suit his views, and then because the towers and other remains do not suit this altered configuration, he changes their names to suit his alterations. Well may Canon Williams have exclaimed: 'Why, at this rate any passage in any book will be sufficient in itself to settle the whole controversy.'

This process of reasoning is used to a very considerable extent, and I will give several instances; but I will now, from the same article, give an instance of his errors by direct incorrect statements.

In order to substantiate his theory, he finds it

necessary to fix the site of Zion, and in order to fix the site of Zion, it is necessary to examine the passages in the Holy Scriptures referring to Zion and Jerusalem, and in doing so he bases his argument on the following very erroneous statement :

'There are also numberless passages in which Zion is spoken of as a holy place in such terms as *are never applied to Jerusalem*, and which can only be understood as applied to the Holy Temple Mount. Such expressions for instance as, "I set my king on my holy hill of Zion "; " The Lord hath chosen Zion "; " Arise ye, and let us go up to Zion to the Lord "; " Thus saith the Lord, I am returned to Zion "; " I am the Lord thy God dwelling in Zion, my holy mountain "; and many others, which will occur to everyone at all familiar with the Scriptures, seem to us to indicate plainly the hill of the Temple. Substitute the *word Jerusalem for Zion* in these passages, and we feel at once how *it grates* on the ear ; for such epithets as these are never applied to that city. On the contrary, if there is a curse uttered, or term of disparagement, it is seldom applied to Zion, but always to her unfortunate sister Jerusalem. *It is never said*, " The Lord dwelleth in Jerusalem," or " loveth Jerusalem," or any such expression, which surely would have occurred had Jerusalem and Zion been one and the same place, as they are now, and generally supposed to have been.'

It will be seen from the above that he attaches much importance in his argument to this, which he asserts to be a fact, and which is stated so positively that I for one, in reading over the article, did not for some time notice how erroneous the statement was. One day, however, when reading it over, it occurred to me that the term, 'The Lord dwelleth in Jerusalem,' or 'loveth Jerusalem,' did *not grate on my ear*, and accordingly I proceeded to test the accuracy of his statement. Then, to my intense surprise, I found it was entirely erroneous, and I first learned to what an extent he lacked accuracy in his writings. On searching the Scriptures I found that Jerusalem shared with Zion the passages referred to, but I will only mention a few instances, sufficient however to unmistakably point out the error of Mr. Fergusson's statement. 'But I have chosen Jerusalem that My name may be there'—'Jerusalem, the city which I have chosen to put My name there'—'House of the Lord at Jerusalem'—'In Jerusalem shall My name be for ever'—'If I forget thee, O Jerusalem, if I prefer not Jerusalem'—'Jerusalem, the throne of the Lord'—'Jerusalem shall be called a city of truth, the mountain of the Lord of Hosts'—'In Salem is His tabernacle'—'Blessed be the Lord out of Zion, which dwelleth at Jerusalem'—'Comfort Zion and chose Jerusalem'—'Pray for the peace of Jerusalem, they shall prosper that love thee'—'And the Lord shall choose Jerusalem again.'

Moreover, I found not only that the Scriptural passages did not prove Zion and Moriah to be one mountain distinct from Jerusalem, but that they on the contrary proved that Zion and Moriah were quite distinct, and this I have shown in 'The Parallel Holiness of Zion and Moriah.' In this it will be seen that Zion is the place of God's name only up *to the date of the transfer of the ark* to the Temple, and that after that, after the building of the Temple, in no single instance in the historical books is Zion called the seat of God's name.

Still quoting from the article 'Jerusalem,' I will point out another class of error in Mr. Fergusson's works. He gives the diameter of the pillars of the Stoa Basilica on the south side of Herod's Temple as 5 feet 6 inches, and placing forty in a row, states that if they were spaced along the southern end of the Noble Sanctuary, it would be necessary to space them at a distance of 23 to 24 feet, which would be architecturally impossible.

Now if we multiply the number of the columns (40) by the spacing *between* the columns, which he asserts will be 23 to 24 feet, we get $40 \times 23\cdot5 = 940$ feet, somewhat more than the total length of the southern side; but there are also the diameters of the columns to be taken into account, so that the spacing will be actually only about 18 feet between the columns, instead of from 23 to 24 as stated by him. This is error No. 1.

I pointed this out to Mr. Fergusson in a letter to the *Athenæum*, but he still adhered to his statement that forty such columns could not be spaced along the south side of the Noble Sanctuary, in accordance with architectural rules.

In this matter I will refute him from his own words, and prove error No. 2.

In his suggested restoration of the Temple of Diana

at Ephesus, previous to the excavations there, he proposes columns about 5 feet 6 inches in diameter, at a distance of 25 feet 7 inches from centre to centre, and states that fifteen columns would cover over 385·7 feet. Therefore forty such columns would extend over 1030 feet (*vide* Fergusson's 'Architecture'), a greater length than the south wall of the Noble Sanctuary. Thus either Mr. Fergusson has made an erroneous statement about the columns of the Stoa Basilica in the 'Dictionary of the Bible,' or else his proposed restoration of the Temple of Diana is *an architectural impossibility.*

Finding eventually that he was in error in this matter, he did not acknowledge it, but in a letter to the *Athenæum*, June 23, 1876, actually imputed to me the proposal of the diameter 5 feet 6 inches, and announced that 'sound criticism' decided 'that the lower diameter of these columns was 3 feet, neither more nor less,' thus suddenly dwarfing the height of the magnificent Stoa Basilica to about half the height he accords it in the 'Dictionary of the Bible.'

* Not content, moreover, with these errors, he attempts to prove that the Stoa could not have extended over the whole length of the south side of the Noble Sanctuary, because the vaults towards the south-east angle are not now strong enough to support them, although he acknowledges that these vaults are a later construction, and even in the 'Temples of the Jews' supposes them to have been built by Constantine, though on the foundations of Solomon's Palace.

* See p. 143.

One would imagine that if they were built in the time of Justinian, there would be no occasion to prove that they could not have sustained these columns of the time of Herod.

Mr. Fergusson's proof, if it is worth anything, is too sweeping; it proves that the Temple never stood in any part of the Noble Sanctuary, because there is no portion of the existing wall on a level with the surface of the sanctuary which was in existence in Herod's time.

I will now proceed to point out rapidly in succession several instances of very remarkable reasoning on Mr. Fergusson's part.

He commences by stating that the Aksa certainly stands on the site of the Jewish Temple, and because it is prophesied in the Holy Scripture that the Temple should be desolate, that *therefore* Justinian did not build his Mary church within its sacred precincts. And if it were not built here, where could it have been built? There is only the space at the south-east angle, therefore Justinian's church is placed at the south-east angle. Now the question is asked, Why did Justinian erect his church 'secus porticum Salomonis'? and the answer is at once, '*Because* the Dome of the Rock was then the anastasis, and because the Basilica of Constantine and the Church of Golgotha were close at hand. And if this be so, then the Dome of the Rock is the identical building which Constantine erected over the Tomb of Christ. And then he goes on to say, 'Lastly, neither Arculfus *nor any historian* mentions this building, unless they describe it as the Church of the Sepulchre.'

Again, he tells us triumphantly that the Aksa Mosque alone was built by Abd el Melek, although the Mahometan historians, who he himself says 'ought to be the best authorities on such a subject,' state that both the Dome of the Rock and the buildings of the Aksa were erected by Abd el Melek. Besant and Palmer even quote a letter written to Abd el Melek at the time, stating this: 'In accordance with the orders given by the Commander of the Faithful, the building of the Dome of the Rock of Jerusalem and the Masjid el Aksa is now so complete that nothing more can be devised.'

How can Mr. Fergusson account for this letter, written at a time when he asserts the Dome of the Rock was in the hands of the Christians as the Holy Sepulchre?

Again Ibn Asâkir, and other Moslem early writers, give the dimensions of the Masjid el Aksa as 755 cubits by 465 cubits, thus clearly taking in the Dome of the Rock, and we know that 'The Jâm'i el Aksa, Jam'i el Magharibe, etc., are *mosques* in our sense of the word, but that the entire Haram is the Masjid' to which the term El Masjid el Aksa is applied.

The whole, therefore, of Mr. Fergusson's reasoning, founded upon this misapprehension of these terms, is of no value.

We have again an extraordinary proposition that the Moslems cast longing eyes on the Dome of the Rock *because* they considered it as the Tomb of Christ, whereas the Moslems do not believe that Christ was crucified or buried, and suppose that a criminal suffered in His place.

We find, again, Mr. Fergusson appealing to Dr. Pierrotti in one part of his book, and in another stating that he has not established his right to be quoted as an authority.

He quotes Sæwulf in his support, and then stigmatises him as an ignorant savage who would believe anything.

He finds the testimony of William of Tyre to be directly contrary to his theory, so he resorts to the very ingenious device of declaring that he was in the plot, and, therefore, must not be believed.

I will now proceed to give in detail my remarks on the erroneous and contradictory statements of Mr. Fergusson.

Mr. Fergusson, in order to substantiate his theory, must prove :

1. That the Temple of Herod was not more than 600 feet per side, and occupied the south-west angle of the Haram area, contrary to all the local indications, historical accounts and traditions.

2. That the original Moslem Sakhra was underground, and not on the surface rock.

3. That the present Moslem Sakhra was not that uncovered by Omar, but was the rock-cut tomb exhumed by Constantine as the site of the Holy Sepulchre.

4. That Constantine built the present Dome of the Rock over the Sakhra, although it is known that Constantine built no dome over the Holy Sepulchre.

5. That between A.D. 870 and A.D. 1100, the Moslems took possession of the Dome of the Rock, the asserted tomb (to Moslems) of Judas Iscariot the criminal, and invested it with the attributes of the true Sakhra.

6. That at the same time the Christians took possession of some other piece of ground, now known as the Holy Sepulchre, built a spurious sepulchre over it, and straightway forgot that it was not the true Sepulchre.

7. That during all the squabbles between Greeks and Latins, Jews and Moslems, Templars and regular clergy, the question of the transference of sites was never mentioned.

8. That the present Holy Sepulchre is not the spot indicated by all the early writers, as the site on which Constantine built his churches.

On the other hand, his theory can be refuted in the following manner:

1. That all local indications, all historical accounts, all Christian, Jewish, and Moslem traditions, prove that the Temple of Herod extended from the west wall of the Noble Sanctuary to the east, from the south wall to the north of the Dome of the Rock platform.

2. That the Dome of the Rock was within the Temple area, and therefore could not have been the sepulchre.

3. That there could not have been ordinary tombs about the site of the Dome of the Rock.

4. That the Dome of the Rock is not a building of the time of Constantine.

5. That Constantine never built any dome over the Holy Sepulchre.

6. That no transference of sites is possible in this case, the historical accounts being so continuous.

7. That Arculf's plan (made in A.D. 680, before the asserted transference) closely resembles the present Holy Sepulchre, and is entirely unlike the Dome of the Rock.

8. That the site of the Sakhra is that which was uncovered by Omar, that it is the traditional site of the Temple among the Jews, and that the Dome of the Rock was built by Abd el Melek.

9. That the present Holy Sepulchre is that which Constantine uncovered, according to all accounts and traditions.

In the following refutation of his arguments, taken in connection with the historical account of the Holy Sepulchre, and paper on the Temple, I believe that I show that he has not proved any one of the points necessary; and, moreover, that he is refuted in all the essential points on which he relied.

SUBJECTS ON WHICH MR. FERGUSSON IS REFUTED.

1. Argument that the Holy Sepulchre was in the present Noble Sanctuary refuted.

2. Position of the Gate of Mahomet shown to vary with several traditions.

3. The proposition of an *underground* Sakhra is purely imagination.

4. Line drawn east and west through his hypothetical underground Sakhra, does not cut the centre of the Wailing-place of the Jews by 75 feet.

5. Line drawn north and south through his hypothetical altar, cuts the true Sakhra as well as the hypothetical Sakhra.

6. The fourth gate does not exist within the 600 feet on the west side, but was found opposite the Sakhra platform.

7. Bridge at Robinson's Arch did not cross the valley, but led into suburbs in the Tyropœon.

8. Gateway under Jam'i el Aksa is only *one* of the Huldah gates; the other is beyond the 600 feet.

9. There was an external gate to the north called 'Tadi,' and therefore Mr. Fergusson's argument about tombs to the north falls to the ground.

10. There is no rock-cutting to the north of his hypothetical temple as there should be, but there is to the north of the Dome of the Rock platform.

11. South-west angle is not part of the old Temple, but was added on by Herod; the ground for 600 feet from the south-west angle is not solid as stated.

12. Buildings at the south-east angle shown to be of ancient date, and not of more modern age as asserted.

13. Statement that the pillars of the great Stoa

Basilica could not have been spaced on the south wall of the Noble Sanctuary refuted from Mr. Fergusson's own works.

14. Wall bounding the Noble Sanctuary on the east side was not built by Herod Agrippa, but by Jewish kings.

15. There is no indication of any break in the sanctuary wall at Wilson's Arch, to accommodate his dimensions for his hypothetical temple.

16. The Turris Antonia is described in history as standing high up on a rock, and not as placed in a hole at the bottom of a valley.

17. Every local indication, contrary to Mr. Fergusson's assertions, tends to show that his hypothetical dimensions of the Temple courts are impossible.

18. Mr. Fergusson makes the same 'unsavoury suggestion' which he twits Professor Willis with having made.

19. Connection between the cisterns of the Noble Sanctuary and the Virgin's Fountain refuted.

20. Statement that neither the altar nor the Temple of the Jews was on a rock, refuted.

21. Statement that the top of the Sakhra was not a threshing-floor proves nothing.

22. Mr. Fergusson proves that the most objectionable site in the whole sanctuary for a temple is that on which he places his own.

23. Mr. Fergusson's argument regarding the position of the altar tells more against his own theory than against any other.

24. He agrees with the rest of the world that the Dome of the Rock is not a mosque.

25. Contrary to his statement, Moslems do turn away from Mecca and face the tombs at which they pray.

26. He agrees that the shape of the Dome of the Rock is suitable to a tomb, and it is pointed out that it covers the Moslem tomb of Solomon.

27. The Dome of the Rock is an oratory erected over the Kibleh of the Moslems, afterwards changed to Mecca.

28. He stumbles among the tombs.

29. And asserts that as it was neither a mosque nor a tomb, that *therefore* it must be the Holy Sepulchre.

30. And must have been built by Constantine, for it is outside the sacred precincts of the Temple, which he limits to 600 feet per side.

31. He asserts that if Constantine did not build it, then architectural science is a delusion, although it is well known that Constantine never did build any dome over the Holy Sepulchre, and although most distinguished architects entirely disagree with Mr. Fergusson.

32. Mr. Fergusson contradicts himself upon architectural subjects connected with the Dome of the Rock, and fails to prove that it is a Christian church.

33. Mr. Fergusson hinges his whole argument as to the sites upon his assertion that a screen in the Dome of the Rock is of the time of Constantine, and fails to prove his case.

34. Dome of the Rock proved to have been built of *old materials*.

35. He asserts that the Dome of the Rock is the most singular building in the whole world, and the reason of this is given.

36. The Golden Gate could not have been the festal entrance of Constantine.

37. No remains of any basilica can be found in the Noble Sanctuary, near the Dome of the Rock, to assist Mr. Fergusson's theory.

38. He makes a distance of 500 feet between his hypothetical Golgotha and Holy Sepulchre, instead of 135 feet.

39. Jam'i el Aksa was originally a Christian church, built by Justinian.

40. Rock from 40 to 60 feet below the surface in some parts of Aksa.

41. Mr. Fergusson confuses the Dome of the Rock and the Mosque el Aksa together.

42. Connection between the Dome of the Rock and the Virgin's Fountain refuted.

43. Position of the Neapolitan Gate proved.

44. Statement of the Innominatus analysed.

45. Date of the visit of Arculf to Jerusalem proved to be about A.D. 680, and not A.D. 700 as stated.

46. Arculf's plan shown to closely resemble the present plan of the Holy Sepulchre, and to be quite unlike the Dome of the Rock.

47. Mr. Fergusson shown to be ignorant of the views of Moslems concerning the Tomb of Christ.

48. So also regarding other tombs of persons who are both Moslem and Christian saints.

49. He cannot suggest any date between the time of Charlemagne and the Crusaders for his alleged transference of the site of the Holy Sepulchre.

50. The Crusaders did not treat the Temple of the Jews with contempt, as stated by Mr. Fergusson.

51. His assertion that the Churches of the Holy Sepulchre have not been burnt or destroyed by the Persians, refuted.

52. Mr. Fergusson at issue with all historians relative to the destruction of the Church of the Holy Sepulchre by El Hakim the Fatimite.

53. Value of the statement of Theodoricus.

54. Mr. Fergusson's statement that Moslems have never built with any kind of ceiled roof, refuted.

55. 'Damning testimony' of Mr. Fergusson exploded.

56. Value of Cufic characters in the Dome of the Rock. Mr. Fergusson again in error.

57. Mr. Fergusson is obliged to abandon his temple of 600 feet per side, and takes one of 585 feet by 610 feet.

58. He accuses me of inaccuracy, and is shown to be inaccurate in his statement, and to have published inaccurate plans.

59. He objects to my proposing that Josephus in one particular instance meant cubits when he said feet, and on the same page himself proposes that where he said cubits he meant feet.

60. He is in a dilemma about the south-east angle of the Noble Sanctuary.

61. He states that my contours are wrong, and is shown to be in error.

62. He suggests that the Jews held a service in an upper-room over the Temple.

1. ['Holy Sepulchre,' p. 51.] 'On the day of the conquest, when the hour of prayer arrived, Omar requested to be conducted to the Mosque of David, that he might pray there, and the Patriarch took him to the Basilica of Constantine, saying "This is the Temple of David;" an expression he could not have used were he speaking of buildings in the town, or the present sepulchre, but is not unnatural in referring to a church so near the Temple as this was, supposing me to be right in the localities I have pointed out.'

Remarks.—This was a natural answer for the Patriarch to have made under the circumstances, with the Holy Sepulchre in its present position, supposing him to have been well acquainted with the Scriptures. The Temple of Solomon was built on Mount Moriah, but the ark in the time of David rested on Mount Zion, and Zion, as the seat of God's name, is most frequently referred to in the Book of Psalms. When, therefore, Omar asked to be shown the Mosque (Masjid, or place of adoration) of David, he was taken to the Basilica of Constantine, built close to the wall of Zion.

2. [H. S., p. 51, *continued*.] 'But Omar replied, " Thou liest ; this is not the place described to me by the Prophet of God," and refused to pray there. He

then proceeded to the Gate of Mohammed,* a perfectly well-known locality south of the Jews' Wailing-place, which was then, as it is now, blocked up nearly to the lintel. Here, creeping in on his hands and knees, he came at last to a place where he could not stand up, and exclaimed : " God is great ; by Him who holds my soul in His hands, this is the Temple of David." '

[Page 99.] ' One of these [gateways] has been discovered, and is now known as the Gate of Mohammed.'

[Page 109.] ' There are two points in this narrative which in themselves ought to suffice to settle the question at issue. The first is that Omar entered the Temple area by the Gate of Mohammed. That gate still exists south of the Jews' Wailing-place, 270 feet from the south-western angle of the Haram area.'

[Page 51.] ' The position of Omar's Rock is clearly marked out by that of the Gate of Mohammed, etc.'

[' Essay,' p. 137.] ' " For if I understand Jalal-eddîn," he proceeds to say, " here is the spot which marks the cleft made by Gabriel, when he found Al Burak outside the house by the Gate of Mahomet," thus making the gateway under the Aksa the Gate of Mahomet, which is further confirmed by the tradition a little further on, where Omar, " when he came at last to the gate called that Gate of Mahomet, drew down all the filth that was on the declivity of the steps of the gate, until he came to a narrow passage," whereas Mejr-ed-din applies this name to the Gate of the Mogribins.'

Remarks.—As Mr. Fergusson lays much stress upon the position of the Gate of Mahomet being well-

* Rendered Mahomet in his later works.

known in former days, and as he upon this assumed position settles in a great measure the position of the Temple, it is necessary to point out that this gate, according to tradition, is located in various parts of the Noble Sanctuary.

Mejr-ed-din says : ' The Bab al Mogharibe ' [to which Mr. Fergusson refers, or rather to the gate beneath it] is also called the Gate of the Prophet,' and after describing the visit of Mahomet on his celebrated night journey, continues: 'Now the Muwakket of Jerusalem have said: "We do not know of a gate in the Noble Sanctuary to which this description is applicable, if it be not that of the Mogharibites."'

Again, he relates of the wicket gate on the east of the Noble Sanctuary, near the Golden Gate : ' This is called the Gate of Burak, because by this gate the prophet entered on his nocturnal journey.' And of the Gate of the Inspector (or Gate of Michæl), on the north-west of the Noble Sanctuary, he says : ' This is the gate to which Gabriel tied the celestial beast Burak on the night of Mahomet's journey.'

Lastly, of the Gate Dawater, on the north of the Noble Sanctuary, he says : ' It is apparently this by which Omar entered on the day of conquest, but God knows best of all things.'

These traditions are still current in Jerusalem, and in the face of them it cannot be asserted positively that the Bab al Mogharibe is the Gate of Mahomet, by which Omar arrived on the platform of the Noble Sanctuary.

And further, if the Basilica of Constantine had been within the present limits of the Noble Sanctuary, as Mr. Fergusson asserts it was, why should Omar have from thence gone *outside* the walls of the Noble Sanctuary, merely in order to scramble in again on his hands and knees through a mass of filth ? Why could he not have walked across the space which then, as now, must have been entirely open ?

Mr. Fergusson in his ' Essay,' page 137, himself gives another traditional position for the Gate of Mahomet, namely, under the Aksa on the south of the Noble Sanctuary.

3. [H. S., p. 51]. ' If we compare the discovery of an underground Sakhra with Eusebius's description of the rock " standing erect and alone in a level space," we at once see how different the two things are. The position of Omar's Rock is clearly marked out by the Gate of Mohammed [refuted in 2], and by other circumstances in the narrative which prove incontestably that it was within the substructures of the Temple. The only doubt that seems possible is whether it was under the Holy of Holies, or under the altar of the Jews. My impression is that the latter is indicated, though this can only be determined by future researches.'

[Page 109]. ' To say that Omar entered there creeping on his hands and knees to look for a rock which " stands out erect and alone," to use the expression of Eusebius—the highest pinnacle of the surrounding localities—is simply absurd. He went to look for the foundations of Solomon's Temple. He entered by the gate nearest them, and found them within the area I have ascribed to the Temple.'

[Page 107.] 'Omar again told him he lied. After which he conducted him to the great church near the gate, called the Gate of the Prophet. Water ran down the steps of the gate, and ran out by the street where the Gate of the City was, in such a manner that the greater part of the steps were below water. The governor then said : " We can only enter here now by creeping." " Be it so," said Omar. Then those that were before Omar and those that were behind him commenced creeping till they came to a plain place [courtyard]. Omar, having looked to the right and to the left, exclaimed : " God is great ! By Him who holds my soul in His hands, this is the Temple of David, from which the Prophet told me he had made the night journey." They found there the rock Sakhra covered with dung, which the Greeks had thrown there in contempt of the Jews. Omar took the corner of his robe, and commenced clearing it, and all the rest followed his example.'

Remarks.—This proposition of an *underground Sakhra* rests only upon Mr. Fergusson's suggestion. Not a hint can be found of this in any account. On the contrary, all history concurs in placing it above-ground and in a prominent position, as it is at present.

The remarks of Mr. Fergusson on Eusebius's testimony are most curious. He has so confused the Rock of the Temple with the Holy Sepulchre, that he actually appears to think that his adversaries are equally confused, and insists that it is absurd to suppose that Omar went on his hands and knees to look for the Holy Sepulchre, which, according to Eusebius, ' stands out erect and alone ;' and *because* such a proceeding is simply absurd, *therefore* the Sakhra he went to discover must be underground.

In other words, having the site of the Holy Sepulchre (A), and of the Temple (B), he transfers A to B and B to an unknown point X (his hidden Sakhra); and then, to confuse the matter still further, states that it is absurd to say that Omar, crawling on his hands and knees after X (an underground Sakhra), should have found A (the Holy Sepulchre) spoken of by Eusebius in the fourth century as standing 'out erect and alone.'

If this is all that can be urged in favour of an underground Sakhra, the case is weak indeed.

Let us examine the levels. The ground-level of the Noble Sanctuary at the south-west angle is 2,420 feet above the Mediterranean: the rock-level of the point where Mr. Fergusson places his Holy of Holies, is probably 2,350 feet; of his altar, 2,410. His proposed Sakhra would therefore have been from at least 10 to 60 feet underground: hence his great anxiety to prove that Omar found a Sakhra underground.

The height of the true Sakhra is 2,440 feet, being 20 feet above the ground-surface of the Noble Sanctuary, and 90 feet above Mr. Fergusson's Holy of Holies.

It is quite natural that a projecting rock, like the true Sakhra, may have attracted the attention of Omar, who had no real knowledge of the exact position of the Temple, and who could only be guided by local indications and the opinion of the residents, which were probably approximately correct; but what possible reason can be adduced for Mr. Fergusson's assertion that he identified some place underground as the 'Temple of David'?

The accounts of the writers on the subject are directly opposed to an underground Sakhra. This is clearly shown in Professor Palmer's translation from Jalal-ed-din:

'So the Patriarch led the way, followed by Omar and the rest of the party, and they crawled along till they came out upon the courtyard of the Temple, where they could stand upright. Then Omar having surveyed the place attentively for some time, suddenly exclaimed: "By Him in whose hands my soul is, this is the Mosque of David, from which the Prophet told us he had ascended into heaven." . . . With these words he stooped down and began to brush off the dung with his sleeve, and his example being followed by the other Mussulmans of the party, they soon cleared all the dung away, and brought the Sakhrah to light. Having done so, he forbade them to pray then until three showers of rain had fallen upon it.'

There are three proofs, then, that the Sakhra was not underground:

1. They came out on 'the open court,' the same name being used as is applied at the present day to the platform on which the Dome of the Rock stands.

2. They cleared away the dung over the Sakhra, until it was exposed to the *light*.

3. They were enjoined not to pray there until it had been washed by three showers of rain.

Thus the account can only refer to a projecting rock, and cannot be made applicable to a rock concealed in the substructures of the buildings.

It is not easy to ascertain from reading the chapter on the subject in 'The Temples of the Jews,' whether Mr. Fergusson still lays so much stress upon an underground Sakhra, or whether, having settled upon another position for it, the necessity for proving it underground is not so urgent.

4. [H. S., p. 112.] 'If anyone will take the trouble of restoring the plan of the Temple of Herod, from the description of Josephus and the Talmud, he will be able to fix the position of the centre of the altar within a few feet either way. Having done this, if he will draw a line east and west through the altar and the Holy of Holies, he will find it cuts the centre of the Jews' Wailing-place. Now we know that the Jews had access to the Temple area in the time of Constantine, and when driven forth, they naturally sought the spot nearest to the Holy Place, to lament over it. They must have known then exactly where it was, and there we find them at this hour.'

Remarks.—The reconstruction of Herod's Temple by Mr. Fergusson is not admitted to be correct. The buildings are all squeezed into the small space he allots to it without due regard to their dimensions given in the Talmud, to which he alludes as one of his authorities.

His own reconstruction of the Temple of Ezekiel, page 83, could not be placed within the limit he assigns to the area of Herod's Temple, without removing the cloisters. And in his reconstruction of the Temple of Herod he has reduced the Court of the Women to about one fourth of its proper size.

Allowing, however, his plan of Herod's Temple to stand for the sake of argument, then his proposition regarding a line through the centre of the Wailing-place, cutting the centre of his altar, is not correct; it cuts about 50 feet north of the centre of his altar.

But the Wailing-place has recently been curtailed by a wall taking a portion of it into the garden of the Mahkama; if, therefore, the line be drawn through the centre of the Wailing-place, as it existed a few years ago, it would cut about 75 feet north of the centre of his altar on the north side of his inner court. It is thus plain that, by Mr. Fergusson's own theory, he has got his altar in the wrong position; it should be 75 feet farther to the north, which alteration would throw out all his argument regarding the Temple having been 600 feet on each side.

We know further from the Rabbins that the wall of the Haram area is considered as sacred under Wilson's Arch and farther north as is the present Wailing-place.

But in truth it is a matter of little moment how nearly this line cuts his altar, for it cannot affect the question either way, both the site of his altar and the limits of the Wailing-place being variable quantities. The Wailing-place happens to be the only available part of the Haram wall where the Jews can wail.

The Jews, when they were turned out of the Noble

Sanctuary, naturally availed themselves of any vacant spot accessible and near the remains of the Temple; but we have no proof that the present Wailing-place was that originally allotted to them. Probably it was not, for there were evidently at one time buildings running along this wall.

All tradition points to the *lapis pertusus* having been near the present Sakhra, and not in the direction of Mr. Fergusson's imaginary altar. The Bordeaux Pilgrim says, 'And not far from the statues is the Beating-stone [*lapis pertusus*], to which the Jews come every year and anoint it, and make lamentations with groans, and rend their garments and so retire.'

5. [H. S., p. 112.] 'If, on the other hand, we draw a line north and south through the same altar, we cut the Kibleh of the Aksa; and according to the Mohammedan authors recording the events of Omar's visit, we find that he ordered the Kibleh to be placed behind the Sakhra, in order that those who pray there may have before them the Kibleh of Mecca, and not that of Jerusalem, because, he added, the Prophet has not ordered us to turn to the Rock Sakhra, but towards the Kaaba. It is, therefore, interesting to find the Kibleh of the Aksa exactly behind the site of the altar of the Jews, and is, amongst others, a tolerable evidence that the site of that altar was known when the mosque was built.'

Remarks.—A line produced north and south through the Mirhab of the Aksa (cutting, as Mr. Fergusson asserts, his altar) passes through the centre of the Sakhra, under the Dome of the Rock, which is thus exactly behind the Aksa where Omar's Mosque was built, and exactly in the position one would suppose it to have occupied from Omar's conversation with his followers.

The accidental position of Mr. Fergusson's hypothetical altar can therefore not be adduced as any strong evidence in its own favour, and certainly cannot be brought forward as evidence against the site of the true Sakhra, which is in one and the same line.

6. [II. S., p. 99.] 'Between these two bridges [Robinson's Arch and Wilson's Arch], Josephus tells us, two gateways led down to the suburb Parbar (Ant., xv. ii. § 5). One of these has been discovered, and is now known as the Gate of Mohammed; the other is probably hid by the buildings of the Mikmeh.'

Remarks.—Diligent search was made for this hypothetical gate of Mr. Fergusson, along the Haram wall behind the Mahkama in 1867-9, from the Bab as Silsile to the Bab al Mogharibe, and the wall was bared at such intervals as will allow it to be positively stated that no such gate exists.

On the other hand, the fourth gate was discovered a considerable distance north of Wilson's Arch, at the Bab al Mathara, leading to Mount Zion, showing incontestably that the Temple area could not have been of the small dimensions given by Mr. Fergusson, and proving that the Dome of the Rock was within the area of Herod's Temple.

This is a matter of so much certainty, that Mr. Fergusson appears to have abandoned this argument, and in his 'Temples of the Jews,' pp. 85, 179, has to resort to the singular confession, that according to the description of Josephus, 'The two Parbar Gates may be anywhere ;' and on this plan he elects to place one of them in his hypothetical Antonia : calling the Parbar Gate that actually was discovered 'Porta Neapolitana,' he with characteristic candour adds : 'And if this is not the true solution, there is little doubt another will reward future investigation.' Which appears to be an admission, that from whatever position he is driven, he will adopt another equally untenable, so long as he has not to abandon his theory that the site of the Temple of Solomon is the Tomb of Christ.

7. [II. S., p. 97.] 'The remains of the bridge [Robinson's Arch] across the Tyropœon, which is coincident with the Stoa Basilica.'

Remark.—This bridge did not cross the valley, it only went down to the suburbs by steps ; there were probably two arches (see 'Recovery of Jerusalem ').

8. [H. S., p. 97.] 'The gateway under the Aksa, which is certainly the double portal near the southern court, mentioned by Josephus.'

Remarks.—It has been shown by Dr. Lightfoot and other authorities, that the two Huldah Gates on the south of the sanctuary were distinct gates, and not one double gate as asserted by Mr. Fergusson. There was a separate guard at each gate, which would not have been necessary had they merely been a double portal. The gate under the Aksa was, no doubt, one of the gates of Huldah; the other, it seems equally certain, was that which is now called the Triple Gate. It has been shown ('Recovery of Jerusalem') that the Triple Gate was, as far as can now be ascertained, originally precisely similar to the Double Gate, having at first only a double tunnel.

These two Huldah Gates divide the southern wall of the Noble Sanctuary, and are apparently the two southern gates spoken of in the 'Tract Measurements of the Temple.'

Mr. Fergusson appears to be unaware that there were two Huldah Gates, for he incorrectly says in 'The Temples of the Jews,' p. 78, when speaking of the Double Gate: 'It is ascertained that they represent the Gate Huldah of the Talmud,' whereas the Talmud says: 'There were five gates to the Mountain of the House, two Huldah Gates in the south which served for going in and out,' etc., showing clearly that they were distinct gates, and not merely one wide passage with columns up the centre.

9. [H. S., p. 129.] 'There was no external gate of the Temple on the north. And Josephus says (Bel., i. v. vii. 3), "while John and his faction defended themselves from the town of Antonia and the northern cloister of the Temple, and fought the Romans before the tomb of Alexander," etc. . . . It is therefore certain that there were tombs at the spot indicated. . . .'

Remarks.—This is a remarkable assertion, rendered necessary apparently in order to prove there were tombs to the north of the Temple, though how the absence of a gate to the north can assist in proving that there were tombs, it is difficult to surmise. The 'Middoth' says, 'There were five gates to the Mountain of the House ; *Tadi on the north* served for no ordinary purpose ;' and again, 'In the gallery that went under the chel he passed out through Tadi ;' and again, ' All the gates there had lintels except Tadi ; there two stones inclined one upon another.' The evidence on the subject points out that Tadi was approached by a tunnel from the inner court of the Temple, and just where it should be, there I have found it, as I have described in 'The Temple.' I there remark, ' We have then the certainty that the passage from Mokad to the House of Baptism was underground, and the inference that Tadi was on the same level and underground also.' Now looking at Dr. Lightfoot's plan, placed over the Haram area, we have already seen that Nitsots is over the passage leading down into the Sakhra, and that there is a passage running in the direction of Mokad, and which appears to unite with Tadi above the northern edge of the mosque platform, at a point where there is a hollow sound as of vaults beneath ; and we further know that there is a scarped rock along at least a portion of the northern edge of the platform.

In 'The Temples of the Jews,' p. 87, Mr. Fergusson admits that there was a Gate Tadi on the north side of the Temple, but fancies it must have been walled up before the siege, in order to strengthen the fortifications ; but he does not mention whether the fact of there having been a gate there, is equally a proof of his theory, as he asserts the non-existence of a gate was.

10. [H. S., p. 130.] 'But Pompey himself filled up the ditch that was on the north side of the Temple, and the entire valley also. In this passage Josephus was speaking of the Temple of Zerubbabel before the Antonia or that of Herod was commenced. The last-named king doubled the extent of the Temple, when the fosse was necessarily filled up and included within the precincts.'

Remarks.—If Mr. Fergusson is right in his dimensions and position of the Temple area, he should be able to point out the position on his plan where the ditch and valley were *before* the Temple was enlarged. This I assert he cannot do, for the rock-ridge can be traced in an unbroken line from the Sakhra to the Triple Gate. On the other hand, I point out this fosse as still being visible on the northern side of the Dome of the Rock platform. This is in itself an overwhelming proof that Mr. Fergusson's position for the Temple is wrong; and the importance of the matter is so apparent to him, that in 'The Temples of the Jews,' p. 69, he is obliged to suggest that Josephus in describing it meant something else. Mr. Fergusson's words are :

'The instances he quotes appear to me sufficient to establish the fact that Josephus believed this to be the case; but it is impossible now to trace its course without excavating under the present level surface of the Haram area, and till that is done, it is of little use insisting on its existence. The only advantage we should derive from knowing its position would be to understand certain rhetorical phrases of Josephus which are now obscure from the want of that knowledge, but which, if taken only for what they are worth, have but little influence on our knowledge of the subject.

11. [H. S., p. 98.] 'If, then, we measure 600 feet eastward from this [south-west] angle, all is practically solid up to that point. Indeed, the living rock can be seen on the surface over the greater part of the Haram area, and in other places can be traced in the underground cisterns extending under the Aksa, and approaching at least within a few feet of the surface.'

['Essay.'] 'A wall does run north and south at right angles with the southern wall, and at a distance of 600 feet from the south-western angle of the Temple enclosure, exactly answering to the description of Josephus, and which I believe most undoubtedly was the eastern wall of Herod's Temple.'

[Page 97.] 'In the first place, no one, I believe, doubts that the south-western angle of the Haram enclosure is one of the angles of the Temple area.'

Remarks.—Here are a series of errors : a glance at the contoured map will show the entire fallacy of Mr. Fergusson's argument ; the statement that the ground for 600 feet from the south-west angle is solid, is absolutely incorrect. The ridge of the rock of Mount Moriah runs upwards in a north-westerly direction, and from this ridge the rock falls to the south-west angle, to a *point one hundred and forty feet below* the level of the Haram area. The south-west angle itself is built right across the *bottom* of the valley by some 80 feet, and the masonry is most decidedly an addition to the original construction, probably of the time of King Herod, and was built when the valley had commenced to fill up, the lower courses being left rough, as they would not be seen : while on the older portions of the wall, the stones are well cut from their foundations. At the eastern end of the 600 feet, at the Triple Gate, the rock is bared, and there is not a vestige of any wall running north and south, as there should be according to Mr. Fergusson's statement ; there is only the remains of the old tunnel similar to the Double Gate, called the Triple Gate (as mentioned in 5), the side of which tunnel is about 585 feet from the south-west angle.

12. [H. S., p. 98.] 'Beyond these 600 feet we come to a range of vaults, unequally spaced, badly constructed, and evidently of much more modern age. On these the Temple could not have been supported, so that in this direction at least, the history and the topography are perfectly agreed.'

Remarks.—The upper portions of these vaults being the reconstruction of a modern date, could not have supported the Temple; but fortunately for the sake of truth, the old wall still remains intact at the south-east angle in all its original magnificence, rising up within a few feet of the level of the Noble Sanctuary, and within this portion are the remains of old vaults of very massive description which did support the Temple cloisters. Moreover, below, on a level with the floor of the vaults and the entrances of the two Huldah Gates, is a row of enormous stones, six feet in height, and running along the face of the southern wall, from the south-east angle to the Double Gate; that at the south-east angle weighing over one hundred tons. Now this huge course extends as far as the Double Gate, and there ends. And this fact, together with the difference of construction of the portions of the wall, shows us that the south-west angle (which Mr. Fergusson asserts to be the old Temple wall) is in fact the more recent portion, probably of the time of Herod, while the portion from the south-east angle to the Double Gate is of one age, probably of the time of Solomon. Here were found the Phœnician characters, painted and incised on the wall, and the pottery jar-handles with Phœnician marks. Here also was found that curious channel under the vaults, which appears to have been the passage for the blood to flow away into the Cedron valley.

It is interesting to find that, after ten years' reflection, Mr. Fergusson has come to the conclusion that the wall at the south-east angle is of ancient date, and that he now agrees with me in ascribing it to the time of Solomon ('The Temples of the Jews,' p. 41): but he still considers that Herod's Temple did not extend so far; and in order to account for the existence of this building at the east of the Temple in Herod's time, he is obliged again to accuse Josephus of exaggeration, and treats as a mere 'rhetorical flourish' his statement that when 'you looked down from the roof of the Stoa you could not see the bottom of the valley, it was so far off.' He omits, however, completely to mention how this palace of

Solomon was used in Herod's time. It surely could not have been left in ruins, and having once admitted its existence, it seems almost impossible to avoid conceding that it formed a portion of the Court of the Gentiles.

13. [Article 'Jerusalem,' p. 1020, Smith's 'Bib. Dict.'] 'Beyond this point [Triple Gate] the Haram area is filled up with a series of light arches supported on square piers, the whole being of so slight a construction that it may be affirmed with absolute certainty that neither the Stoa Basilica nor any of the larger buildings of the Temple ever stood on them. The proof of this is not difficult. Taking Josephus's account of the great Stoa as we find it, he states that it consisted of four rows of Corinthian pillars, forty in each row. If they extended along the whole length of the present southern wall, they must have been spaced between 23 and 24 feet apart, and this, from our knowledge of the works of the ancients, we may assert to be architecturally impossible. But far more than this, the piers that support the vaults in question are only about 3 feet 6 inches by 3 feet 3 inches square, while the pillars which it is assumed they supported were between 5 and 6 feet in diameter (Ant., xv. 11, § 5), so that, if this were so, the foundations must have been practically about half the area of the columns they support. Even this is not all: the piers in the vaults are so irregularly spaced, some 17, some 20 or 21, and one even 30 feet apart, that the pillars of the Stoa must have stood in most instances on the crown or sides of the arches, and these are so weak (as may be seen from the roots of the trees above having struck through them), that they could not for one hour have supported the

weight. In fact, there can be no doubt whatever that the buildings of the Temple never stood on this frail prop, and also that no more solid foundations ever existed here, for the bare rock is visible everywhere; and if even more solidly built upon, the remains of such constructions could not have disappeared. In so far, therefore, as the southern wall is concerned, we may rest perfectly satisfied with Josephus's description that the Temple extended east and west 600 feet.'

Remarks.—* This astounding statement has been practically abandoned by Mr. Fergusson; but as he, in a letter to the *Athenæum* of July 20, 1875, states that he has not changed his views on a single important point since he first published on the subject, and as this has been considered a very important point, if substantiated by him, I find it necessary again to point out his errors as briefly as possible, more especially as he states ('The Temples of the Jews,' note 2, p. 75), that he completely refuted me on this occasion, and that I have since tried to forget all about the subject.

The term he makes use of, 'between 23 and 24 feet *apart*,' in this passage can only mean 'between 23 and 24 feet from centre to centre,' as the length of the southern wall (923 feet) will not admit of any other application of those figures; thus the intercolumniation to which he takes exception would be 18 feet, and not 23 to 24 feet (as stated by him), that is, a little over 3 diameters, or diastyle, using columns 5' 6" in diameter, as proposed by him.

* See p. 113.

I do not know on what grounds he pronounces such dimensions in this particular case to be 'architecturally impossible,' but I can point to his conjectural plan of the Temple of Diana at Ephesus, in which *he* suggests a spacing of 25 feet 7 inches from centre to centre of columns, giving, even with the somewhat greater diameter adopted, an intercolumniation of *over* 18 feet.

On this being pointed out by me in a letter to the *Athenæum* of June 20, 1875, Mr. Fergusson abandoned the diameter of 5 feet 6 inches, which he had proposed in his article 'Jerusalem,' and declared that 'sound criticism' would not allow of such a diameter, and that 'the lower diameter of these columns, according to Josephus, was 3 feet, *neither more nor less.*'

In order to do this, he is obliged to entirely alter the text of Josephus, and to suppose a transposition of terms ('The Temples of the Jews,' p. 81); and even then he gets into further difficulties, and throws over the text altogether, imagining what Josephus ought to have said if the Temple area had been but 600 feet per side. But as it is only necessary to fit Josephus's dimensions into the true length of the outer court of the Temple, it is not necessary to follow up his assertion. Suffice it to point out that, according to the text of Josephus, the columns of this southern cloister should have been about 5 feet 6 inches in diameter; that in Mr. Fergusson's 'History of Architecture,' p. 245, he spaces the columns in his restoration of the Temple of Diana at Ephesus at 25 feet 7 inches from centre to centre, so that 40 such columns would extend over a length of 1,030 feet, whereas the south Haram wall is only 923 feet in length.

I do not know what is to result from Mr. Fergusson's effort to prove that the columns of the Stoa Basilica could not have stood on the 'weak vaults' which he himself states were built by the Emperor Justinian ('The Temples of the Jews,' p. 247). That they could have stood on the older foundations of Solomon's palace there can be no doubt, for portions of this massive masonry can still be seen. Mr. Fergusson's statement 'that no more solid foundations ever existed here' than those weak vaults, is now of little value, since he has allowed that this ground may have been occupied by Solomon's palace.

14. [H. S., p. 58.] 'It is necessary to explain that the wall which now bounds the Haram area on its eastern side was built by Herod Agrippa, twelve years after the crucifixion.'

Remarks.—The wall of Herod Agrippa is described by Josephus (Bel., v. 4, § 2) as joining the *old wall* on the east side of Jerusalem. This east wall of the Noble Sanctuary is the *old wall*, on which the porch of Solomon stood in the time of Agrippa, and therefore cannot be the wall built by Agrippa. At its base, both north near the Birket Israel and south at the south-east angle, were found the Phœnician characters on the stones. It is still in parts over 200 feet in height, and is one with the south sanctuary wall. At the south-east angle the Ophel wall is found to abut, as is described by Josephus.

The discovery of the Ophel wall at this point is in itself sufficient to destroy Mr. Fergusson's theory, but he is obliged to still insist that the old east wall was built by King Agrippa, *after* the crucifixion, in order that the ground about the Dome of the Rock may be proved to have been open country at that time.

15. [H. S., p. 98.] 'Again, if we measure 600 feet northward from this [south-east] angle, we come to a second bridge, an arch of which is said to have been discovered by Lieutenant Wilson.'

Remarks.—There is no indication whatever near this bridge of any termination of the Temple wall at 600 feet from the south-west angle, as asserted by Mr. Fergusson. On the contrary, we know that it exists at several points in the same line up to the present north-west angle, and the presumption is that it still exists in one unbroken line throughout the length of the present west wall of the Noble Sanctuary; and if so, it is difficult to understand how Mr. Fergusson would propose to deal with this wall.

16. [H. S., p. 59.] 'The Turris Antonia I believe all admit was the Prætorium, or residence of the Roman Governor. And no one doubts that it stood at the north-west angle of the Temple, near where the Mekmeh now stands.'

Remarks.— The Turris Antonia is everywhere described as being on a *high rock*, which was scarped, whereas the Mekmeh stands over the lower part of the Tyropœon valley, where the bottom is about 80 feet below the level of the Noble Sanctuary. The Antonia could not have stood in this valley and have guarded the Temple, if it stood on a rock. Mr. Fergusson must either again abandon his position, or again alter the text of Josephus. He gives no reason for putting the citadel of the Temple at the bottom of the valley.

17. [H. S., p. 100.] 'Every indication on the spot tends to show that the Temple of Herod was, as Josephus tells us, 400 cubits or 600 feet square, and was situated, as marked on the plan, in the south-western angle of the Haram area. Since then the rock, which now stands under the Dome of the Rock, is situated nearly 800 feet from the southern wall ; it was certainly outside the area of the Temple, at a distance of 150 feet from its northern wall.'

Remarks.—The local indications, on the contrary, all appear to point to a Temple area of about 900 to 1,000 feet a side, and every indication mentioned by Mr. Fergusson appears to assist in destroying his theory.

The arguments in favour of a Temple area which included the Sakhra are so numerous, that we can do no more than enumerate some of them.

Josephus tells us repeatedly that the Temple was placed on the *top* of a hill (and not in the hole to which Mr. Fergusson assigns it). I have shown in another place that we are not bound to 600 feet per side for the Temple area ; that this was the size of Solomon's Temple, and that Herod's Temple area was doubled. The west, south, and east walls are still *in situ*, and the north wall has recently been discovered on the north of the Dome of the Rock platform, where Mr. Fergusson places his hypothetical Basilica of Constantine. The west, east and south walls (except a portion at the south-west angle which appears to be of the time of Herod) have the appearance of having been erected in the earliest times, being built up with fair faces from the foundations; and on the east wall have been found Phœnician characters. In the south wall are the two Huldah (Double and Triple) Gates. Below the single gate has been found the passage for carrying off the blood. At the south-east angle abuts the wall of Ophel. The east wall is that on which the porch of Solomon still stood in the days of the Apostles. The Golden Gate being on the foundations of the Gate Shushan, through which the Red Heifer was conducted to Olivet. On the west side are the four gates leading to the suburbs at Robinson's Arch and Bab al Mogharibe, to the Upper City at Wilson's Arch, and to the Akra or Zion by Bab Mathra.

In the north wall, on the northern side of the Dome of the Rock platform, is the Gate Tadi, leading through a tunnel to the Gate Nitsots under the Sakhra. The Sakhra is the Chamber of the Washers, and the Gate Mokad is in the prolongation of a passage or tunnel (now used as a tank) in which was the House of Baptism, leading to Tadi and Antonia on the rock north-west of the Noble Sanctuary. There is a valley and fosse between it and the Temple.

It is impossible in so small a space to do justice to the great number of small local indications which all point to but one position for the Temple. They will be found discussed in the 'Recovery of Jerusalem,' 'Underground Jerusalem,' and the 'Quarterly Statements of the Palestine Exploration Fund.' What I have to point out here is principally the system of errors in which Mr. Fergusson has involved himself, owing to the position he has taken up.

18. [H. S., p. 100.] 'I need hardly stop to point out that this determination at once gets rid of all those theories which would place the altar of the Temple on the rock, even if their untenableness could not be easily demonstrated from other circumstances; and above all, it frees us from the incubus of Professor Willis's unsavoury suggestion, which would make the Bir Arroah into a cesspool, and convert the Pool of the Virgin, the sacred fount of Siloam, and all that is poetic and beautiful in " the stream that flowed fast by the oracle of God," into so many reservoirs of liquid manure.'

Remarks.—This may be a 'rhetorical flourish' only, for it is difficult to understand what Mr. Fergusson really means by his reference to Professor Willis's 'unsavoury suggestion,' as he appears to make exactly the same suggestion himself as to the great rock-cut reservoirs in front of the Aksa: from which there are water channels running into the Kedron, and which are also connected with the other tanks under the Dome of the Rock.

It is obvious that the blood must have been carried

away from the altar by some underground passages (Middoth), and why Mr. Fergusson should object to the space under the Sakhra being used for the blood any more than the space under his hypothetical Sakhra, is not apparent.

However, as the Sakhra was not the altar, and was not (so far as we know at present) connected with the Pool of Siloam, this is not a very material matter, beyond exhibiting the weakness of Mr. Fergusson's case.

19. [H. S., p. 50.] 'Now this connection between the cisterns in the Haram area and the fountains of the Virgin and Siloam had long been suspected, but only recently established by the exploration of Dr. Barclay and Dr. Pierotti, and no such connection exists between the localities on the opposite hill and these fountains. This, therefore, is one of those pieces of unconscious testimony which are so valuable in cases of this sort, where there can be no mistake and no motive, and which consequently ought to be considered final, until some new facts get rid of their " damning testimony."'

Remarks.—Mr. Fergusson very much mars the value of his 'damning testimonies' by telling us (p. 129) that Dr. Pierotti has not established his right to be quoted on this or any other subject.

Major Wilson, in 1866, established the inaccuracies of Dr. Pierotti in this matter; and later investigations have established the certainty that the sewer that Dr. Barclay explored does not find its way into the

Virgin's Fountain. It was a portion of the main drain of the city that he explored, and at the present day it is again in use, and can be seen discharging into the Kedron valley. It has no known connection with the Noble Sanctuary, and comes down the Tyropœon valley.

20. [H. S., p. 101.] 'Before leaving this branch of the subject, it would be well to inquire where it is said that the altar of the Jews was placed on a rock. It certainly is not mentioned in the Bible, or in Josephus, nor in the Talmud, nor in any other authority to which we usually apply on such occasions. What we know of the altar is that it was first of brass and then built of small stones, on which no tool had been passed.'

[Page 20.] 'But it need hardly be remarked that the word "rock" does not occur either in the Bible, or in Josephus, or in the Talmud, nor indeed anywhere else in ancient times, as connected either with the altar or Holy of Holies. It seems to be wholly a Moslem tradition, but has been repeated so often in the present controversy that most persons have come to believe that there is some foundation for the belief that this rock represents the site of the altar, though there does not seem to be any whatever.'

[Page 20.] 'What we know from Josephus is that the altar was built up of natural unhewn stones, which no iron tool had touched (B. J., v. 5, § 6), and the Talmud repeats this even more distinctly and positively (Middoth, iii. 4), so that there is absolutely no authority except the modern tradition for connecting the altar and *the Temple* with any rock.'

[Page 63.] 'The only reason ever advanced by anyone for assigning it [the dome of the Rock] to them [the Moslems] being that on that rock stood the Holy of Holies, or the altar of the Jews.'

Remarks.—Mr. Fergusson states that there is no authority except modern tradition for connecting the altar or *the Temple* with any rock. This assertion can readily be refuted.

Threshing-floors in Palestine are made of dry clay in the plains, and of flat portions of rock in the mountains. As the whole of Mount Moriah is of a hard rocky nature, it may be stated with absolute certainty that the threshing-floor of Araunah the Jebusite was a portion of that rock. The altar being placed on the threshing-floor, it must have stood on the rock. Josephus is very clear on this point (Ant., viii. 3, § 9), 'When Solomon had filled up great valleys with earth, and had elevated the ground four hundred cubits, he made it to be on a level with *the top of the mountain on which the Temple was built*, and by this means the outmost Temple, which was exposed to the air, was even with the Temple itself.'

Again (Bel. Jud., v. 5, § 1), 'Now this Temple was built upon a strong hill. At first the *plain at the top was hardly sufficient for the Holy House and the altar*, for the ground about it was very uneven, like a precipice.'

The following account is only applicable to a rocky mount. Ezekiel xliii. 12 : 'This is the law of the House. Upon the top of the mountain the whole limit thereof round about shall be most holy.' The Talmud states this even more positively and distinctly, regarding the 'aven shiteyeh.' Dr. Chaplin, in summing up the Talmudic evidence, states, 'The teaching of the Talmudic doctors therefore indicates clearly that the 'aven shiteyeh' was rock, and not a detached stone, projecting three finger-breadths from the floor of the Holy of Holies, covering a cavity which was regarded as the mouth of *the abyss*, reverenced as the centre and foundation of the world, and having the ineffable name of God inscribed on it.

Although it is not contended (by me) that the Sakhrah was either the site of the altar or Holy of Holies, it is yet interesting to find that the Mahometans have exactly the same tradition regarding the Sakhra as the Jews had, as to the rock in the Holy of Holies. Yet in spite of this evidence, Mr. Fergusson states that there *is absolutely no authority in the Bible, Josephus, or Talmud, for connecting the altar or Temple with any rock.*

It is somewhat startling to find that Mr. Fergusson, in 'The Temples of the Jews,' p. 36, appears to place his hypothetical altar upon the rock, stating that his temple stands on a ridge of rock. He is, however, quite incorrect in stating that his temple, in its hypothetical position, would stand upon a ridge of rock : it would stand in a hole, and it is only necessary to examine his plates to be certain of this.

21. [H. S., p. 101.] 'And as for its [the altar's] site, it was placed in the threshing-floor of Araunah. Now the rough rock beneath the Dome certainly

never was nor ever could have been a threshing-floor.'

[H. S., p. 20.] 'What we know of the altar from the Bible is that it was situated on the threshing-floor of Araunah, and this rugged and uneven rock certainly never was and never could have been a threshing-floor under any circumstances.'

[H. S., p. 101.] 'In fact, turn which way you will, the Sakhra was not the site of the Jewish altar, and never could have been.'

Remarks.—It is not contended that the Sakhra was the altar, but that it was the rock over the cave Parva, where (it is related in the Talmud) a magician digged a vault underground till he could come to see what the high priests did on the day of expiation; and that over this was the 'chamber of the washers,' in the northern portion of the inner court of the Temple. In early days the corn was garnered into caves near to the threshing-floors, and it has been suggested by Dean Stanley that the cave under the Sakhra was used for such a purpose, and that within its recesses Araunah hid himself on the memorable occasion of the visit of the angel.

All late Jewish and Mahometan writers concur in supposing the Sakhra to have been the Holy of Holies, and not the altar.

22. [H. S., p. 101.] 'But besides this we know that the site of the altar was lower than the floor of the Temple.'

As threshing-floors are generally so placed on the

ridge of a hill as to catch every breath of air (when the winnowing is in progress), it would appear probable that the rock on which the Temple was built was necessarily a little lower than that on which the altar was built, owing to the shape of Mount Moriah; the floor being raised up to the required height. Of this matter little can yet be said, but at least on one point we may be certain (from examination of the ground), viz., that if this objection of Mr. Fergusson is valid, then the most objectionable site in the whole Noble Sanctuary for a Temple is that on which he has located the Temple of Herod.

23. [H. S., p. 101.] 'If the altar had been placed on this rock [the Sakhra], and the Temple erected between it and the Tyropœon valley, its substructures must have been so gigantic that it is almost impossible they should have disappeared as they have done.

'In fact, turn which way you will, the Sakhrah was not the site of the Jewish altar, and never could have been. 1st. It was outside the Temple [according to Mr. Fergusson's theory]. 2nd. The rock theory is a mere Mahometan tradition [see 19], which has been adopted without thinking; and lastly, there is no site for the Temple behind it, while every indication on the spot contradicts such an hypothesis. On the other hand, if we place the altar where shown in the plans given above, and assign to the Temple the limits and the site there shown, every local peculiarity agrees with such a position, while every historical deduction confirms the local indications.'

Remarks.—The substructures no doubt were gigantic, history assists us so far. It is, however, worthy of remark, that if built on the rock with the Sakhra as the site of the altar there would be a difference of fifty feet in height between the rock at the altar and the Holy of Holies. If built in the portion I assign to it, only twenty feet between ; but if built in the position where Mr. Fergusson locates it, there would be the enormous difference of *seventy feet* in height between the rock at the altar and the Holy of Holies. So that this argument of Mr. Fergusson (if of any value) tells more against his own position than against any other.

Again he states that there was not room for the Temple behind the Sakhra as the site of the altar ; but his own altar is at the same distance from the west sanctuary wall as the centre of the Sakhra, and the rock from his altar falls to the west much more rapidly or steeply : therefore, if there was not room for the Temple behind the Sakhra, *à fortiori* there was not room for the Temple behind his hypothetical altar.

24. [H. S., p. 67.] 'I had visited the mosques and tombs of Cairo and Egypt, and had acquainted myself with those of Persia, Syria, and Asia generally, in so far as was possible from the books then published; but in all my researches one building alone stood out strange and incomprehensible, and that was the so-called mosque of Omar, at Jerusalem. Mosque it certainly was not, for in its arrangements it transgressed the fundamental principle of mosque architecture. The essential definition of a mosque, reduced to its simplest expression, is that it is a wall at right angles to the direction of Mecca.'

Remarks.—Mr. Fergusson himself states (p. 18), 'The octagonal building *popularly* known as the Mosque of Omar, but more correctly termed the Dome of the Rock;' and again (p. 115), 'The name as applied to the Dome of the Rock is simply a mistake of the Christians; by Mahometans, that building is known as the Kubbet es Sakhra, or "Dome of the Rock."'

As it is well known that its popular name is a misnomer, and that Christians alike agree in acknowledging its name to be 'the Dome of the Rock,' built by Abd el Melek, why does Mr. Fergusson introduce the question as to its being a mosque?

As well might he go through the form of proving that the so-called 'Mosque of Hebron' is not a mosque. The rectangular building there containing the cenotaphs of the patriarchs is not a mosque in the popular sense of the term, it is an oratory, or makam, similar to the other Mahometan welis, or saints' tombs, about the country. The real Mosque of Hebron is adjoining the old building containing the cenotaphs. So at Jerusalem, the Dome of the Rock is the weli, and the Aksa and other praying places (towards Mecca) are the mosques. It is therefore useless, for the sake of any real argument, to attempt to prove that the Dome of the Rock is not a praying place for the Mecca Kibleh. Mr. Fergusson's object, however, in this matter will be seen from the sequel, his argument being, 'and if it is not the Mosque of Omar, it must be the church of the Holy Sepulchre, built by Constantine.'

25. [H. S., p. 6.] 'Now the building in question [Dome of the Rock], so far from answering to this description, is an octagon, and with an entrance in each of the four faces fronting the cardinal points of the compass, but strange to say, with the principal entrance facing the south, or direction of Mecca, so that every worshipper entering by it turns his back on the Holy Kaaba, a sacrifice which anyone who has lived long among Moslems will easily feel and appreciate.'

Remarks.—Mr. Fergusson quite misunderstands the habits of the Moslems of Arabia, however well he possibly may be acquainted with those of India.

The Arabian Moslems frequently turn away from Mecca and face the tombs at which they pray. How much more so will they be inclined to do this when praying at either of the two places on earth which share with the Kaaba the honour of being considered portions of Paradise, viz., the *Sakhra at Jerusalem* and garden at Medina !

'When praying at the tomb of Mahomet they face the tomb, *with backs to Mecca.*'—Burton's ' Mecca.'

Again, ' It is best for anyone entering the Sakhrah to do so on the right hand, so that he may have *his back towards the sacred processioners around the Kaaba.*' —' Jalal-ed-Din.'

There are plenty of praying places or mosques within the Noble Sanctuary where faithful Moslems may perform their ordinary periodical devotion towards Mecca ; but when pilgrims (who come specially to Jerusalem for the purpose) are within the Dome of the Rock they usually have to consider the awful associations of the venerable rock which they behold—a portion of Paradise on earth—a rock which is only second to the Kaaba itself, which was the original Kibleh, and which has twice since been the Kibleh in lieu of the Kaaba.

26. [H. S., p. 7.] 'Had it been called the *Tomb* of Omar, I probably should hardly have inquired further. Tombs in the earliest ages of the world were circular. They afterwards became octagonal, and sometimes square, and generally after the Roman period were surmounted by domes, as this building.'

[Page 1030, '*Bib. Dic.*,' Smith.] 'Had it been called the Tomb of Omar, this incongruity would not have been apparent, *for all the old Moslem and Christian tombs adopt nearly the same ordinance.*

['Essay,' p. 111.] 'There are octagonal tombs, it is true, though not many, and only, I think, in India; but this the Mahometans *never called a tomb*, nor connected any such idea with it.

Remarks.—Surely this is mere playing with words. The Moslems do not call it a mosque, and do call it a tomb. Mr. Fergusson states very positively that the Moslems have never called it a tomb, nor connected any such idea with it, but he cannot be supposed ignorant of the fact that the Sakhra is, with the Moslems, the *Tomb of Solomon.*

Indeed, in 'The Temples of the Jews,' p. 57, he actually says, 'It is curious to find that Solomon's sepulchre is still pointed out under the Dome of the Rock, on the north side of the Sakhra.' It would be interesting to know how Mr. Fergusson will account for these contradictions.

But the Sakhra has a far greater claim to be domed over, than as being the Tomb of Solomon, for it is the centre of the world, the gate of heaven, paradise on earth, etc. (see 27). If a tomb therefore deserves covering with a dome, how much more so this venerable rock, uniting all the most transcendent qualities calculated to make it dear to the Moslem mind!

Mr. Fergusson makes an admission in stating that domed buildings, of the plan of the 'Dome of the Rock,' came into use *after the Roman period*, to cover sepulchres. Here we have such a building covering such a sepulchre (of Solomon), and something more than a sepulchre; it may therefore, according to his admission, have been planned after the Roman period, and consequently by the Moslems.

27. [H. S., p. 7.] 'I had seen hundreds, I may almost say thousands, of Moslem tombs in the East, differing in no very essential respect, in so far as plan is concerned, from this one. Many had four entrances, but generally, it must be confessed, the door facing Mecca was closed, and ornamented with a mirhab, or niche of prayer; but this was not an essential, and certainly not always the case.'

Remarks.—Mr. Fergusson may also see hundreds of similar places of prayer in Palestine:

'As M. de Vogüé has pointed out, the Cubbet es Sakhra, notwithstanding its imposing proportions, is not, properly speaking, a mosque, and is not constructed with a view to the celebration of public prayers and services. It is only an oratory, one of the numerous *cubbehs* with which the Haram es Sherif abounds—domed edifices that mark the spots to which tradition clings. The form is, in fact, almost identical with that of an ordinary Moslem *weli*, or saint's tomb. El Jám'i el Aksa is, on the other hand, a mosque designed expressly for the accommodation of a large congregation assembled for public worship, and resembling in its architectural details the celebrated mosques of Constantinople or elsewhere.'—Besant and Palmer's ' Jerusalem,' p. 85.

28. [H. S., p. 7.] 'Though, therefore, it might in the then state of our knowledge have been classed among the tombs, there unfortunately was no tradition or hint of any kind that either Omar, or any saint or celebrity [what was King Solomon?] had been buried beneath its dome.'

[Page 44.] ' In the next place it is the most singular building in the whole world ; no other edifice, either Christian or Saracenic, is built over a living rock which occupies the whole of its floor, which is in fact the cause and object of its building ; and even if it could be shown that a hundred or a thousand ordinary churches were erected in Palestine at that age, this consequently would still have been the most remarkable.'

[Page 21.] ' The whole floor is occupied by a large mass of living rock, rising about eight feet above the level of the aisles, and in that rock is a cave, regarding the rise and origin of which the Moslems are by no means clear.'

[Page 114.] 'The Temple of the Jews was a sacred spot to the Moslems, because their Prophet had started thence on his night journey to heaven, and had noted it with honour and reverence in the Koran. They also respected it because they hoped at that time to rally the Jews under their standard, and to convert them to Mahometanism.'

Remarks.—Even as regards its being the tomb of a Moslem saint, Mr. Fergusson is wrong; for the Dome of the Rock is over the Sepulchre of King Solomon (according to Moslem tradition), and he certainly is a Moslem 'saint or celebrity' equal to David, Samuel, Hosea, Jonah, and others whose sepulchres (or supposed sepulchres) are covered over and jealously watched.

But, as previously stated, the Sakhra has a sanctity in the eyes of the Moslems even greater than a tomb. Being in their eyes the site of the Temple of Solomon, they have invested it with many of the attributes with which the Jews surround the Holy of Holies. It was the first Kibleh for prayer instituted by Mahomet, and so far enjoys an advantage even over the Kaaba itself. Mahomet himself said, 'The first of places is Jerusalem, and the first of rocks is the Sakhra.' It is the centre of the world, and is eighteen miles nearer heaven than any other portion, and will exist forty years after the remainder of the world is destroyed. It is Bethel, the gate of heaven, and is suspended miraculously between heaven and earth, and is on the top of a palm tree, from the roots of which spring all the principal rivers of the earth. It is one of the three portions of paradise on earth, and has impressions upon it of the footsteps of the Prophet, the hand-print of the angel Gabriel, and about it are the praying-places of Elias and the prophets.

It was from this rock that the Prophet ascended the ladder into heaven on his celebrated night expedition. There is not another spot on the face of the earth to which so many wonderful legends are attached. Then surely this venerable rock, which Mahomet designed to be the centre attraction of Islam, which in the time of Abd el Melek was the centre of attraction and Kibleh of the Moslems—surely this stone deserves a covering far more beautiful than that surmounting the tomb of a Moslem saint, than that covering the tomb of one of the 124,000 Moslem prophets, or even than those of the great prophets.

And it did receive its reward, for Abd el Melek erected over it a building of old materials, nondescript of order, but beautiful to view. This building, much altered, is now the Dome of the Rock.

29. [H. S., p. 7.] 'If therefore it was neither a mosque nor tomb, what was it? My knowledge was at fault, and I could suggest no answer.'

[Page 115.] 'If then the Dome of the Rock was not built by the Saracens, it must have been built by the

Christians: there was no third party in the field who could have done it. If this be so, I would ask again, what church did Constantine or any other Christian priest or monarch build in Jerusalem over a great rock with one cave in it, but the church of the Holy Sepulchre?'

Remarks.—There is something almost comical about the dilemma within which Mr. Fergusson has involved himself, in order to give a greater colouring to his account of his discovery of the Holy Sepulchre under the Dome of the Rock.

He proves, where no proof was required, that the Dome of the Rock was not a mosque; shuts his eyes to the real position it held (notably that of a *cubbeh*), and in his necessity grasps at the extraordinary notion that it is a Christian church, built over the Holy Sepulchre by Constantine.

Truly a fitting sequel to his former series of arguments, for it is well authenticated that Constantine 'built no church over the sepulchre at all' (Besant and Palmer).

What Constantine did do at the true and present site of the Holy Sepulchre was to decorate the cave magnificently, to pave over the court around which was open to the sky, and to build a basilica to the east on the site of the Crucifixion and Invention of the Cross. There is not the slightest intimation of any dome or building over the sepulchre until after the destruction of the churches by Chosroes and the rebuilding by Modestus.

30. [II. S., p. 8.] ' " And who do you suppose built

it?" "Omar." "Omar!" I exclaimed: "it is impossible he can have done so. This is a Christian Sepulchre of the time of Constantine. It can be no other than the Church of the Holy Sepulchre."'

[Page 128.] 'El Hakim did burn and destroy the Basilica of Constantine, sometimes called the Church of the Holy Sepulchre, and no trace of it is left except in the Golden Gateway; but there is absolutely no hint in any author, Christian or Mahometan, that I know of, that the Moslems either burned or destroyed the Anastasis or Tomb of Christ.'

['Essay,' p. 102.] Church of the Holy Sepulchre. 'This church was then, as long afterwards, called the Martyrium, or testimonial, in contradistinction to the other, or round church, called the Anastasis, or Church of the Resurrection, from its containing the sepulchre from which Christ arose on the third day. The former did not apparently stand over any holy spot or place.'

Remarks.—It is an interesting study to observe the mental process by which Mr. Fergusson arrived at this remarkable result. In 1846 he was looking over the drawings of the Dome of the Rock, and seized by a sudden impulse, he exclaimed, 'It can be no other than the Church of the Holy Sepulchre.' Since then he has made all facts of every description, and however antagonistic, do duty in his service, and help to prove his theory. Even the statement of Eusebius, in the fourth century, that the sepulchre, when cut from the cliff by Constantine, 'stands out erect and alone,' is cited (pp. 51 and 109) to prove that Omar, in the seventh century, found the Sakhra underground.

He appears to reason that because (as he asserts) the Dome of the Rock is the Holy Sepulchre, therefore it must have been without the sacred precincts of the Temple, therefore the true Sakhra is near the Aksa, therefore the present Sakhra is not the true Sakhra; and if so, what is the Dome over it? It can be nothing else but the Church of the Holy Sepulchre. This completes the circle, and the argument commences again with variations.

31. [H. S., p. 27.] 'If, in short, Constantine did not build this Dome of the Rock, our architectural science is a delusion, unless some one can bring forward new data from which new conclusions must be drawn.'

Remarks.—Mr. Fergusson here constitutes himself the mouthpiece of architectural science, quite ignoring the number of professors on the subject, who declare this building is not of the time of Constantine. It is difficult to understand how, with any justice to the science, he can speak so positively, when Professor Willis and the Count de Vogüé entirely disagree with him. He has not brought forward the testimony of a single architect who can support his reasoning on architectural grounds, which, in itself, is a significant fact; and though he himself is acknowledged to be a forcible exponent of his own doctrine, he can scarcely expect his readers to give to his individual dogmatic and unsupported opinion the deference which would be given to those of professional architects.

32. [H. S., p. 26.] 'The whole arrangement and

design of the building is utterly unlike anything we know of Saracenic architecture, and there is a beauty of proportion and appropriateness of detail which we do not find in their works till their style was thoroughly elaborated into a whole after the Crusades.'

[H. S., p. 30.] 'This would be apparent at a glance to everyone if it were not that the Dome has been used as a place of worship for fifteen centuries, first by Christians, then by Mahometans. During the Crusades the Christians recovered it, and made it the Patriarchal Church of Jerusalem, and again the Mahometans adapted it to their own rites. It has been so altered by all these changes in many of its details, that the original form and construction are not at once apparent.'

['Essay,' p. 109.] 'On the other hand, the Dome of the Rock is of a very beautiful design, *complete and uniform in all its parts and details*; and this no Mahometan building is that I know of till the period when they abandoned the employment of *borrowed classical detail*, whose use they did not understand.'

[H. S., p. 21.] 'The central dome is supported by four great piers, between each of which there are three pillars supporting arches springing direct from their capitals. Beyond this, the external space of thirty-five feet is divided into two aisles by a screen of eight piers and sixteen pillars, and nearly 400 feet in length, which is the most interesting *and most unaltered part of the building, and that consequently on which the architectural argument mainly hinges.*'

[H. S., p. 24.] 'Anteriorly, perhaps, the best for the purpose is the octagonal temple or tomb building above alluded to, which Diocletian erected in his palace at Spalatro. It is, in all essential respects, identical with this building at Jerusalem, except that the first-named emperor, like a good pagan, put his colonnade outside his building in the form of a peristyle, while Constantine, like a good Christian, put his inside, in the shape of an aisle.'

Remarks.—The views given in these five paragraphs are somewhat discordant. We are first told that the arrangement and design of the building is utterly unlike anything known to be Saracenic, although at p. 7 (No. 27) he has informed us that hundreds or thousands of Moslem tombs in the East differ in no very essential respect, in so far as plan is concerned, from this one. He admits therefore that the plan may be Saracenic.

What, therefore, does he mean by the arrangement and design of the building, for he also admits that the screen of eight piers and sixteen pillars 'is the most unaltered part of the building, and that consequently on which the architectural argument mainly rests'? Again, he tells us that the building has been so altered by the changes of the Christians and Moslems, that the original form and construction are not at once apparent, and also that it has a beauty of proportion and appropriateness of detail which we do not find in the works of the Saracens, till their style was thoroughly elaborated into a whole after the Crusades. So that he admits that the proportion and detail may have been the work of the Saracens after the time of the Crusades, and at the same time tells us that the original form and construction are not at once apparent. Surely this appears to be practically a complete surrender of his remarkable theory.

He allows the place is Saracenic, that the construction and details are also Saracenic, with the exception of the peristyle, which M. Ganneau has proved to be made of old materials; the beauty and appropriateness belong to that of a building adorned by the Saracens about the time of the Crusades (Mr. Fergusson says after the Crusades). All this he admits is apparent at the present time, but yet if the Dome had not been in the hands of Moslems and Christians so many years, it would be seen at a glance that it is of the date of Constantine.

As though to make this strange argument still more strange, we are told by him that the Dome of the Rock is in all essential respects identical with the temple of Diocletian at Spalatro, except that Diocletian, 'like a good pagan, put his colonnade outside his building in the form of a peristyle; while Constantine, like a good Christian, put his inside in the shape of an aisle.' Had Mr. Fergusson ventured to give a view of the temple of Diocletian alluded to, instead of giving merely the courtyard of the palace, the hollowness of his reasoning would have been at once apparent.

33. [H. S., p. 23.] 'We have thus in this building, in the centre, circular arches resting directly on the capitals, as at Spalatro [as also in Saracenic and Christian buildings of the twelfth century]. We have in the screen arches resting on an entablature supported by architrave blocks; but we have not the

third stage, which became universal in the fifth century, and continued generally throughout Justinian's reign, of arches springing direct from the architrave blocks without any intervening entablature.

'Look at it, indeed, which way you will, it is impossible to conceive a more essentially transitional example than this, the horizontal trabeate of pagan Rome struggling to retain its position against the Christian arcuate style, by which it was so soon to be superseded. After this period, as far as I know, there is not a single instance of a horizontal cornice being used as a decorative feature anywhere. It died with Constantine, and we here witness its last expiring agony.'

Remarks.—As Mr. Fergusson states that his architectural argument mainly hinges on the screen forming the peristyle or aisle, that alone will be alluded to.

The matter is very simple. In the building at Spalatro, of the second century, the arches spring direct from the capital without any intervening entablature; in the buildings of Justinian, of the sixth century, the arches spring from the capitals or architrave blocks without any intervening entablature; therefore he assumes that the discharging arches of the screen in the Dome of the Rock, resting on an entablature supported by architrave blocks, must belong to a date between the second and sixth centuries. This is strange reasoning indeed, especially when he cannot adduce a single example of this kind at so early a date, and even has the rashness (so far as his theory is concerned) to write, ' *The mode in which the entablature is used here is peculiar, perhaps unique*

... for though, as for instance in the Baptistery of Constantine at Rome and elsewhere, we have such an entablature running over a lower and above an upper range of pillars, *I know no instance of a discharging arch being used as this is.*—' Essays,' p. 104.

This reasoning may be shown to be still more unreasonable, when we find that a nearly similar feature, in the Mosque el Aksa, is put forward by Mr. Fergusson as an argument against 'its late Roman origin, and a convincing proof of its Mahometan origin.'

In the Mosque el Aksa the discharging arches rest on the entablature which is supported by the capitals. It seems probable that this feature in the screen of the Dome of the Rock, which Mr. Fergusson asserts (without a shadow of a reason) to be of the last expiring agony of the architecture of pagan Rome (time of Constantine), is distinctly Moslem of the seventh or eighth century. The materials, as will be pointed out hereafter, have undoubtedly been used a second time.

34. [H. S., p. 22.] 'The first thing to be remarked in the screen is that the pillars are mounted on stools or sub-bases, as in the octagon building of Spalatro, and as we find them in the buildings of the next century at Salonica and Constantinople, but as they ceased to be in Justinian's time and afterwards.

'The capitals are of a simple Corinthian order of Diocletian's day, which had disappeared long before Justinian's reign. Above them still range the old classical entablature, but with this remarkable alteration. Although of wood, it would have looked crushingly heavy if maintaining its classical depth across pillars spaced eight diameters apart. The architrave is consequently omitted, and represented only by a square block over each pillar, supporting the frieze and cornice, of fairly classical design, and over this cornice a bold discharging arch, which again supports a cornice which was originally apparently classical, but is now hid in more modern details.'

Remarks.—Lieutenant-Colonel Wilson states that the Dome of the Rock has been so frequently repaired and covered by various decorations, that it is difficult to say what belongs to the original building ('Ordinance Survey Notes').

In 1874 opportunities arose for examining the bases of columns of screens; and M. le Comte (a French architect) took advantage of these circumstances for making valuable notes.

M. Clement Ganneau, 19th March, 1874, writes from Jerusalem about this screen, or intermediary peristyle, he having had access to the notes of M. le Comte, and assisted him in his observations:

' A glance at the drawing will show the form of the bases better than any description. It suffices to show one important fact—*that they are heterogeneous* . . . . they vary in every case absolutely from the base E, as much in the dimensions as in the description of the mouldings. Finally, the marble in which they are cut is not of the same kind for each. The aspect of the bases fully confirms (what the variety of modules in the columns above might teach us) the opinion of those who see in the original building ancient materials from various sources used over again.

'This use, which seems very improbable in ancient work, even of late period, is, on the contrary, quite in accordance with Arab customs. It is clear that if these bases and columns, whatever their absolute age, had been made specially for the Cubbet es Sakhra, they would be all alike.'—'Palestine Exploration Fund,' 1874, p. 153.

We have thus, it is clear, in the Dome of the Rock a Saracenic plan, with Saracenic arrangement and details, a distinctive feature of their work being the screen or intermediary peristyle, which is constructed of old materials, columns of different sizes and lengths, and bases heterogeneous. The capitals of the columns alone appear to be identical in character, and are said to be similar to those in the Basilica at Bethlehem; so that they may have been brought over from Constantine's Basilica on Olivet, after the destruction by Chosroes.

The details of capital and entablature are well given by De Vogüé in 'Le Temple de Jérusalem;' but after close examination no trace could be found by M. le Comte of the Cross which he supposes to have been cut upon them.

Thus it appears, that with the exception of the more modern portions, everything about the Dome of the Rock is essentially Saracenic in arrangement, that the materials where ancient are not *in situ*, and that there is not a shadow of reason for Mr. Fergusson's assertion that the building must date from the time of Constantine.

35. [II. S., p. 25.] 'It need hardly be added that in those days retrogression in style was absolutely unknown, and those who contend that this building was erected by Moslems, or by any other parties after the time of Justinian, have got to point out the existence of any one building in any part of the world, or in any subsequent age, which resembles this one either in design or style. Such a building may exist, but of this I feel certain, that it has not yet been seen by modern eye, or at least described by modern pen; and we may treat *de non apparentibus* as *non existentibus*.'

Remarks.—Mr. Fergusson's answer refutes the above statement at page 44 of the same book as follows:

'In the next place, it is the most singular building in the whole world: no other edifice, either Christian or Saracenic, is built over a living rock, which occupies the whole of its floor, *which is in fact the cause and object* of its building; and even if it could be shown that a hundred or a thousand ordinary churches were erected in Palestine at that age, this consequently would still have been the most remarkable.'

In this endeavour to show the Dome of the Rock to be over the Holy Sepulchre, he proves too much for his own purpose. He only shows most forcibly how undoubtedly the Moslems have conveyed the traditions of the Jews regarding the site of the altar and Holy of Holies to the Dome of the Rock, it being to them the centre of the world, the gate of heaven. Merj-ed-din and Jalal-ed-din (to whose authority Mr. Fergusson appeals) most fully describe the building of the Dome of the Rock, and entirely refute his theories that it was built by Constantine.

Professor Palmer, the eminent Arabic scholar, states: 'It must be distinctly understood that Arabic historians are as clear and explicit as to the building of this splendid Dome as we should be on the building of St. Paul's by Christopher Wren.'—Besant and Palmer's 'Jerusalem,' p. 487.

Mr. W. Simpson, in his paper on the 'Transference of Sites' ('Palestine Exploration Fund,' 1879, p. 28), states : 'If the architecture of the Dome of the Rock permitted of the theory that it was built by Mahometans, the only supposition that would explain it would be that it was constructed as a Kibleh, like the Kaaba, which is not any ordinary mosque, and changed afterwards.' This is exactly what did occur. Again he says, 'The arrangement of the building is identical with so many Oriental tombs, and strikingly so with all the principal tombs of India.'

36. [H. S., p. 34.] Golden Gate. 'It is not, and from its arrangements could not be a gate of the city. It was not and could not be a gate of the "accursed Temple" of the Jews, which did not extend nearly to this spot, and which certainly was not rebuilt in the fourth or fifth century. If, therefore, it was not either of these, which could it be but the festal entrance described by Eusebius, as leading to the Basilica of Constantine?'

Remarks.—If, as Mr. Fergusson states, it was not a gate of the city, how could it be the festal entrance described by Eusebius, as opening on to the very middle of the market-place in the Akra? There is no indication of anything of the kind in front of the Golden Gate, and no possibility of a market having been held there.

As it certainly was not the festal entrance of Constantine, so on the other hand does it appear probable that it was, before its reconstruction, the East Gate of the Temple Court, the Gate Shushan. The old foundations and columns are still visible, similar to those in the Triple Gate in the South Wall. After the destruction of Jerusalem it appears to have been rebuilt on its old foundations, and to have been used as a city gate. Omar is said to have closed the gate, 'and it only opens at the end of the world, when Jesus the son of Mary shall descend upon the earth. It seems they were closed for fear, and to secure the Haram enclosure and the city, because it faces the desert, and there could be no advantage in leaving it open (to facilitate the entry of the Bedawin).' This account appears to be an echo of that given in the book of Ezekiel, regarding the East Gate of the Temple.

37. [H. S., p. 35.] 'No remains now exist of the Basilica to which the Golden Gate led. Some of the pillars which once adorned it are no doubt to be found among those forming screens, and decorating buildings in the Haram area or elsewhere; and some portions of its cornice are used as a string course in the façade of the present Church of the Holy Sepulchre, but nothing remains *in situ*.

'One circumstance, however, may be mentioned as

bearing on the site of the Golden Gateway. In describing the Basilica, Eusebius speaks of the side aisles "as well those underground as those above ground;" meaning evidently thereby that the upper galleries were approached on the level, from the outside, like those of the nearly contemporary Church of S. Lorenzo and Sta. Agnese at Rome. The fact is interesting here, as it accounts for the position of the Golden Gateway, some fifteen feet below the level of the Haram area—a circumstance which it would not be easy to account for without reference to this fact, but which is just one of those numerous confirmations that are sure to spring up when the investigation is on the right tack.'

Remarks.—Mr. Fergusson has truly stated the case when he says that no remains exist of the Basilica of Constantine near the Golden Gate; and an inspectioy of the ground will show that Constantine's Basilica can never have existed there. Mr. Fergusson appears to have abandoned the position which he originally assigned to the Basilica (*vide* the 'Temples of the Jews'), in consequence of my discovery of the northern scarp of the Temple Courts on the northern edge of the Dome of the Rock platform, and now places it on the outside of that scarp. This new site, however, is quite as objectionable as that which he originally assigned, for the rock crops up to the surface just where he places the atrium, so that he must search again for some new and more convenient site.

There is only one spot, however, where the Basilica is likely to fit in, and that is to the east of the present

Holy Sepulchre, where the remains of the portal still exists, and where it may have stood half in and half out of the rock (according to his translation), and facing the market-place.

It is unfortunate, however, for the one of Mr. Fergusson's unconscious and 'damning testimonies,' that another translation of this passage from Eusebius says nothing about the Basilica being built in the rock; it runs: 'Besides this were two porticoes on each side, with upper and lower ranges of pillars, corresponding in length with the church itself.'

The account of the buildings about the Sepulchre, given by Eusebius, is diametrically opposed to the views entertained by Mr. Fergusson, who, while quoting from him when it is convenient, ranks him as 'last of the historians,' though 'not quite first of the fabulists.'

The description exactly accords with the present position of the Holy Sepulchre, as has been shown previously.

The fact of the propylea opening direct upon the market-place, is sufficient to refute the proposition that it could have been on the site of the Golden Gate. There is no broad space in front of that gate sufficient for a market, which, moreover, Josephus informs us was held in the Akra, which was close to the present site of the Holy Sepulchre. The account of the New Jerusalem having been erected around the Sepulchre, over against that one, so infamous of old, is indicative of its having been erected north-west of the Akra, divided by deep valleys from the Upper City and Mount Moriah, as is described by Josephus.

38. [H. S., p. 53.] 'Between the Sepulchre and the Church of Golgotha was a large place, the dimensions of which we get from Antoninus, who says it measured 400 feet. And in this, it is added by Arculfus, was the place where Abraham erected his altar for the purpose of slaying his son Isaac, a locality always, before the Crusades, connected with the vicinity of the Temple, and never supposed to have occurred in the town.'

Remarks.—It is not clear how Mr. Fergusson arrives at the conclusion that Antoninus measured '400 feet' between the Sepulchre and Golgotha; the term used appears to be 'gressus lxxx.,' and eighty paces of thirty inches each (the usual length of a pace) gives only 200 feet. The actual distance in a straight line from the centre of the tomb to the place where the cross is supposed to have been erected, measuring through the walls, is 135 feet. But the Pilgrim could not have measured in this manner; the shortest distance he could have made it, pacing on the ground, is 185 feet, a very close approximation to what he gives. Mr. Fergusson's plan, on the other hand, from his hypothetical tomb to his hypothetical Golgotha, gives 500 feet, which, if the Pilgrim strided in eighty paces, he would have taken five feet to a pace. There are few men in these days who can make such bounds.

It is not known how Mr. Fergusson arrives at the conclusion, that previous to the Crusades the vicinity of the Temple was always connected with the place where Abraham erected his altar for the purpose of slaying Isaac, or what bearing it has on the argument.

39. [H. S., p. 37.] 'Whoever built it, of this fact we may be certain—that two or three centuries at least elapsed between the erection of the Dome of the Rock and the Aksa, and that the latter is the more modern. It would be as reasonable to assert that the naves of Rochester and Canterbury—as we now find them—were erected by the same architect, in the same age, as to ascribe those two buildings to one time.

'At the same time the evidence, both architectural and historical, is amply sufficient to prove that the Aksa was built by Abd el Melek ibn Merwan, and finished in the year 72 Hegira, A.D. 791' [should be 691].

[Page 38.] 'The great difficulty which Justinian experienced in building his church, and the wonder of it when accomplished, was, according to Procopius, the vaulted substructure which he was obliged to erect in order to get a level place on which to build his superstructure. Now the substructures of the Aksa, in so far as they are of masonry, are of Herod's time, and not erected by Justinian at all.'

[Page 38.] 'There is no apse to the plan, and neither the details nor the ordinance of the Aksa are those of Justinian's other buildings; nor, indeed, those of the Christian church, though not unlike those of the mosque at Cordova and other Moslem buildings of that age. It never would have been assumed to have been built for Christian purposes had its arrangements been studied with care, and with the view of assigning them their true place in the series.'

Remarks.—The expression used by Mr. Fergusson regarding the naves of Rochester and Canterbury Cathedrals, as we now find them, exactly explains away the difficulty he is in regarding the difference of style between the Dome of the Rock and the Mosque el Aksa. He will readily acknowledge that these cathedrals are not the same now as when originally built, but as to the Aksa Mosque, because it differs now in style from the Dome of the Rock, therefore it cannot originally have been built about the same period. The fact is, it has been built and rebuilt at several periods. First we may see the old double tunnel, one of the Huldah Gates of the Temple, extending 190 feet from the south wall. Beyond these vaults we find a further extension of them to a distance of seventy-five feet, making 265 feet from the south wall, to support the Church of Justinian (which Mr. Fergusson, without any valid reason, and without proof, asserts was not built here). After this church was destroyed by Chosroes in 614, the site was occupied by Omar's building, and was fully covered by extensive erections of Abd el Melek. These buildings, however, fell to decay. Merj-ed-din tells us that in the days of Abu-Jafar-Almansur-al-Abbassi (A.D. 755), 'The eastern side of the mosque hath now fallen; and the western side fell at the time of the earthquake, the year one hundred and thirty [A.D. 748].' 'Then there was a second earthquake, and the building which Abu-Jafâr had commissioned to be built fell down. Then afterwards Al Mahidi acceded to the throne [A.D. 770 ?], and the mosque was in ruins, which being reported to him, he commanded it to be rebuilt, and said, This mosque was narrow and long, and was deserted of men, diminish its length and augment its width; and it was finished in his Khalifat.'

Professor Palmer also tells us that in the year preceding A.D. 831, 'Jerusalem also profited by Mamûn's peaceful rule and æsthetic tastes, and the Haram buildings were thoroughly restored. So completely was this done that the Masjid may be almost said to owe its present existence to El Mamûn; for had it not been for his care and munificence, it must have fallen into irreparable decay.'

It is thus apparent why the Dome of the Rock and the Aksa Mosque are not alike in style.

'This mosque [el Aksa] is universally regarded by Oriental Christians, and also by the Frank Catholics, as an ancient Christian Church, once dedicated to the Virgin.'—Robinson, sec. vii. p. 297.

40. [H. S., p. 38.] 'But the greater part of the building rests on the rock, which crops up to the surface in some places within it, and in others is only a few feet below the surface.'

Remarks.—Mr. Fergusson is again exceedingly in error in thus implying that the greater part of the

Aksa rests on the rock. The rock is only known to crop up to the surface at the north-east angle. On the western side it is from forty to sixty feet below the surface of the Noble Sanctuary, and the substructures must extend upwards from that depth.

41. [H. S., p. 38.] 'In addition to this negative evidence, we have the positive and repeated assurance of the Mahometan historians, who ought to be the best authorities on such a subject, that the Aksa was built by Abd el Melek.

'They give its dimensions, and describe its details with a minuteness which leaves no doubt as to their meaning. Thus Jelal-ed-din says, "There are in the mosque fifteen chapels to match the chapel of the Sakhra." There are just seven spaces on each side of the Aksa, and the chapel opposite the Mosque of Omar would complete the number.

'And again the same authority says, "The Mosque el Aksa is divided into seven compartments, supported by piers and columns, among which forty-five are columns, and thirty-three pillars," which is the exact number given in Catherwood's plan, and numerous other details are given, which leave no mistake as to the building they are describing.'

['Essay,' p. 139.] 'Merj-ed-din says the Aksa "is divided into seven compartments, supported by columns and piers, among which forty-five are columns, of which thirty-three are of marble, and twelve of common stone; the thirteenth column is at the eastern gate, near the altar of Zacharias. There are altogether forty piers of common stone.*"'

* 'An enumeration which is singularly confirmed by Mr. Catherwood's plan.'

Remarks.—Mr. Fergusson can produce no authority whatever for thus confounding and confusing the two buildings, the Dome of the Rock and the Mosque el Aksa.

The Mahometan historians, as he himself observes, ought to be the best authorities on the subject, and they always distinguish between the Dome of the Rock and the Mosque el Aksa : it is Mr. Fergusson alone who confuses them together. The Mahometan historians give a most precise account of both structures; and as they wrote in the fifteenth century, when Mr. Fergusson must allow they were as distinct as they are at present, it is quite impossible that they can be talking of the Aksa alone.

As to the number of the columns and piers being the same now as they were in the fifteenth century, it surely can scarcely influence the subject. I do not think, moreover, that if any ten persons were to count the piers and columns as they at present exist, any two results would be similar, many of the columns being engaged to the piers.

But if the number of columns could be cited as a proof, then it goes against Mr. Fergusson's theory, and is also a remarkable example of his power of finding a coincidence when he wants one.

In 1847 he tells us that Merj-ed-din states there were forty-five columns and *forty piers*, which he (Mr. Fergusson) remarks is singularly confirmed by Mr. Catherwood's plan. In 1865 he tells us that Jelal-ed-din states that there were forty-five columns and *thirty-three* piers, which he (Mr. Fergusson) again discovers is the exact number given in Catherwood's plan.

That is to say, the forty piers of Merj-ed-din are to be found in Catherwood's plan in 1847, and the thirty-three piers imputed to Jelal-ed-din are to be found in the same plan in 1865. Truly Mr. Fergusson might have acted on the advice he is so liberal in tending to others, and have called the assistance of an architect or draftsman 'to aid him in reproducing his ideas in a form which would render them intelligible to others.'

As they at present stand, his system of argument is ably summed up by Canon Williams in two lines: 'Why, at this rate, any passage in any book will be sufficient in itself to settle the whole controversy.'— 'Holy City,' vol. ii. p. 103.

42. [H. S., p. 49.] 'In the same age we have a curious piece of circumstantial evidence, which in any court of law would probably be considered final. A traveller, Antoninus Martyr, after describing the Holy Places, adds: "Near the altar (of the Church of Golgotha) is a crack or opening *(crepatura)*, where if you place your ear you hear the flowing of water; and if you throw in an apple, anything that will swim, and go to Siloam, you will find it there." Now this connection between the cisterns in the Haram area and the fountains of the Virgin and Siloam had long been suspected, but only recently established by the explorations of Dr. Barclay and Sig. Pierotti.'

Remarks.—It has already been shown (18) that there is every evidence against the connection of the cisterns in the Haram area and the Virgin's Fountain, and Mr. Fergusson himself, on p. 129, states that his principal authority 'has not established his right to be quoted as an authority on this or any other subject.'

The story of the apple, as told by Antoninus Martyr, appears to be somewhat imaginative, and yet it is almost certain that there was an aqueduct running from the Jaffa Gate down to Siloam by the Tyropœon valley, between Golgotha and the Upper City; but whether this water-course was in any way connected with the site of the Crucifixion, it is not possible at present to say. The evidence, however, whatever it may be worth, is entirely against Mr. Fergusson, and is another of his 'damning testimonies' which have turned against him.

43. [H. S., p. 48.] 'In the itinerary of the Bordeaux Pilgrim we have another contemporary record of what was then (A.D. 333) being done at Jerusalem, but unfortunately so indistinct that it is impossible to make much of it. Those who adduce his evidence in favour of the present building, maintain that the Porta Neapolitana is the Damascus Gate, but without any authority for such an assumption beyond the fact of Nablûs being north of Jerusalem. On the other hand, it seems more logical to believe that this was the gate of the New Jerusalem just alluded to, in which case his testimony is final in favour of the views I am now contending for.'

Remarks.—Mr. Fergusson acknowledges (p. 9) that the position of the Neapolitan Gate is an historical difficulty which goes against his theory ; and it certainly is as much against it now as ever, yet he seems to wish to make it do duty in his favour whether it will or no.

He would have us suppose that the mere fact of Nablûs being north of Jerusalem was not enough in itself to give the gate the name of Neapolitana : how does this accord with the fact that even to the present day the gates and streets of villages and towns are usually named after the towns towards which they point or lead. Nay, even the very gate corresponding to it at the present day is called the Damascus Gate, because it leads out towards Damascus, just as in the palmy days of Neapolis, or Nablûs, it would have been called the Neapolitan Gate.

There is, however, another reason why this gate may have been so named. It was in the second wall opening out upon that portion of Bezetha enclosed by the third wall, and called Cœnopolis, or the New City. Mr. Fergusson even goes so far in another passage ('Essay,' p. 92) as to say that this position of the city was called Neapolis by Josephus; but here he has made a misquotation, for Josephus does not make use of a compound word, he only says ' New City.'

There is also a third reason why this gate should be called Neapolitana, viz., that it led to the New City built by Constantine around the Holy Sepulchre.

Take any of these reasons individually, and the whole collectively, and it will be found that but one direction for this gate is indicated, and that Mr. Fergusson is again in error. There is no escape for him this time from the difficulty he has admitted, the evidence on which he states is final. It is clearly stated by the Bordeaux Pilgrim that this gate was in the north of the city. This Pilgrim, after seeing the palace of David (present Cœnaculum) within the Upper City, went without the wall (first wall) towards the Neapolitan Gate to the north, and saw on his right hand the Prætorium, and on his left Golgotha, about a stone's throw (forty yards) from the Sepulchre. On this spot, he informs us, the Emperor Constantine was erecting a basilica, which was in course of construction at that very time. This account cannot possibly be accommodated to Mr. Fergusson's views.

44. [H. S., p. 9.] 'The first extract from the description of our anonymous traveller settles the long-disputed question of the site of the Porta Neapolitana. This was the *only historical difficulty* that really existed, which, though not important in itself, was still sufficiently so to render its removal satisfactory.'

[Page 119.] 'The point which makes the MS. valuable is the fixation of the "Porta Neapolitana." The Prætorium of Pilate certainly was the Turris Antonia. At all events, even those who contend for the present tradition must admit that it was eastward of the Arch of Ecce Homo. The Porta Neapolitana, which was attached to it, must consequently have been one of the gates of what is now known as the Haram area, and the testimony of the MS. seems equally clear that the Church of Golgotha and the Anastasis were then within that sacred enclosure. In so far as such evidence can decide a case of this sort, it appears to be conclusive, and ought to be considered as final.'

Remarks.—Of all the strange reasons adduced by Mr. Fergusson in favour of his hypothetical position for the Holy Sepulchre, this is one of the most peculiar.

The statement of an anonymous author (not traveller, as stated by Mr. Fergusson), writing from whence we know not, and living at an unknown period, and most certainly in his account mixing up buildings of the fourth and twelfth centuries, is taken to prove that the Neapolitan Gate is one of the gates of the present Noble Sanctuary; whereas, if the MS. is of any value whatever, it most distinctly proves that the Neapolitan Gate was the northern gate of the second wall of the city, between the Prætorium and Golgotha. And further, it proves that the Temple area was then, as it is now, two bow-shots to the east of the Holy Sepulchre. The description given by this anonymous author was published by Dr. Titus Tobler, from a codex in the British Museum; and with Dr. Tobler I quite concur in thinking that it is a compilation of accounts, and that the first portion of the description mentions buildings as they existed before the attack of Chosroes, for it is most clearly a condensed account of that given by the Bordeaux Pilgrim (A.D. 333), while the other appears to be a condensed account of Sæwulf.

After leaving the Temple area he follows the steps of the Bordeaux Pilgrim to the house of Caiphas in the Tyropœon valley, under the Upper City. Thence passing over to the Palace of David (the present Cœnaculum) in the Upper City, he again follows the Pilgrim, and says : ' Towards the Neapolitan Gate is the Prætorium of Pilate, where Christ was judged by the chief priest; thence not far off is Golgotha,' etc. A glance at the map will show that in this he follows and agrees with the Bordeaux Pilgrim. .

The remainder of the account appears to me to bear unmistakable traces of being a condensed account of Sæwulf (A.D. 1103), while Dr. Tobler thinks that the whole account was written in the eleventh century.

The following extracts from the account are almost literal translations of the text of the Innominatus, and if they are of any real value, completely overthrow Mr. Fergusson's theory and prove him to be hopelessly in error; for he places the Temple of the Lord to the east of the Holy Sepulchre, at a distance of two arbalist-shots, exactly in the relative position they occupy at present, while Mr. Fergusson, in his hypothetical sites, places the Temple to the south of the Holy Sepulchre, at not half an arbalist-shot :

' We descend from our Lord's Sepulchre, about the

distance of two arbalist-shots, to the Temple of the Lord, which is to the east of the Holy Sepulchre . . . the place where Solomon built the Temple . . . here the Lord Jesus . . . was received by the aged Simon. . . . . In the Court of the Temple of the Lord, to the south, is the Temple of Solomon, of wonderful magnitude. . . . Towards the north . . . is the font called in Hebrew Bethsaida, having five porticoes [piscina probatica].'

Who can doubt that this is an account of the present Holy Sepulchre and present Haram area? the Innominatus must most assuredly consider the present Dome of the Rock to be the *Templum Domini*, and the Aksa the Temple of Solomon. It follows then that, according to him, the Prætorium must have been near the north-west angle of the present Noble Sanctuary, where it was supposed to have been by writers of the twelfth century, and the Neapolitan Gate between it and Golgotha, as shown on the map.

45. [H. S., p. 110.] 'There is only one other quotation with which I need trouble you at present. Arculfus, the French bishop whose account of the Holy Place is the most distinct and complete we have, tells us that, "In that famous place whereon the Temple was constructed with great magnificence, the Saracens have erected a square house of prayer on the remains of some ruins, which house may contain 3000 persons."

'As this was written certainly eight years after the year 72 Hegira, when Abd el Melek is said to have completed the Dome of the Rock, it proves that the

Saracens had not at that time broken the treaty Omar had made with the Patriarch Sophronius.

'Had the Saracens erected also the Dome of the Rock at that period, it seems impossible that Arculfus could have omitted to mention it, as the chief and by far the most important building of the two. Besides this, there is no whisper that the treaty with Omar had been broken or infringed. All that had then been done had been to build the Mosque el Aksa, which stood within the precincts of the Temple, which had been assigned to the Saracens by the treaty.

'Unless, indeed, we can put on one side the whole account of the Holy Places, as given by Arculfus, it amounts to as absolute a proof as could well be afforded, either that the Dome of the Rock was described by him under the denomination of the Anastasis, or that it did not exist when he was at Jerusalem in the year 700.'

Remarks.—Mr. Fergusson, before he can attempt to substantiate this argument, must prove that Arculf was at Jerusalem as late as A.D. 700. He will have some difficulty in doing so, although he says it is a matter of certainty, for I can prove from Mr. Fergusson himself that Arculf could not have visited Jerusalem later than A.D. 698, the true date of his visit being about A.D. 680.

Mr. Fergusson states that the account was certainly written eight years after the year 72 Hegira; that is, in A.D. 699.

As it was written the winter after Arculf returned from Palestine, it is difficult to comprehend how Mr. Fergusson can make out that it was written *before*

Arculf visited Palestine, which he states was A.D. 700.

But it is not two years, but twenty years that I must take away from the date on which he states Arculf was in Jerusalem.

We find ('Biographia Britannica Literaria,' Anglo-Saxon period, p. 202) that Adamnan visited the court of the Northumbrian king, Aldfrid, at least as early as A.D. 701, and then presented to the king his book on the Holy Places, 'which he had taken down from the dictation of the Bishop Arculf,' but we have no proof that this occurred immediately after Arculf's long visit; and when we think of the long time taken in writing, copying, and illuminating old books, it is in a high degree improbable that Arculf's visit could have taken place in the previous year.

Arculf, however, himself settles the question, so far as we are concerned, for he is made to say in his narrative, 'Majuvias, Saracenorum rex, qui nostra ætate fuit, judex postulatus.'

Now Majuvias, or Moaweyeh I., reigned from 661 to 679, and Moaweyeh II. reigned during the year 683.

So that Arculf's visit must apparently be placed during one or other of these reigns; it is not material which, as the Dome of the Rock was not commenced until A.D. 684.

Abd el Melek commenced his reign A.D. 684, and died 705; he commenced the Dome of the Rock 684, and completed it 691.

During this period, owing to Mecca being in the

hands of a rival, he made the Sakhra the Kibleh and centre of attraction of the Moslems under his rule. Jerusalem was therefore in an exceptional condition during his reign, and it would seem impossible that Arculf could have visited at that time and have made no mention of the magnificent Dome then in course of construction. His account must evidently be referred to one of the preceding reigns, before the Temple area received the grand addition of Abd el Melek, and his own statement regarding King Majuvias clearly shows that it was at Jerusalem in or before the year A.D. 683.

46. [H. S., p. 52.] 'Arculf, the French bishop, who visited Jerusalem in the end of the seventh century, and described the Holy Places with a minuteness surpassing all other authors of that epoch.

'He not only described the four churches of the Christians, but gives a plan, a "vile figuration," as he modestly calls it, which, if taken in conjunction with his text, enables us to understand clearly what he means, and to prove incontestably that he was not speaking of one church containing all the localities under one roof as we now find them.

'First, he describes the Anastasis, or round church, containing the sepulchre; secondly, the square Church of St. Mary; third, another very large church on the east of the sepulchre ("per grandis ecclesia orientem versus"), called the Church of Golgotha; fourth, the Basilica or Martyrium, constructed by Constantine with grand magnificence.'

Remarks.—The plan given by Arculf is so very similar to the present plan of the buildings about the

Holy Sepulchre, and so very unlike the plan of the Dome of the Rock, that Mr. Fergusson has to resort to an ingenious, singular, and most characteristic argument, as follows :

['Essay,' p. 154.] 'Let us, then, assume that the Christians were turned out of their original sepulchre and Golgotha by the Mahometans. Nothing can be more improbable than that they had a correct plan of the localities . . . but here they had one, and when compelled to transfer their sepulchre to a new locality, can anything be more probable than that they should take the plan known to all the Latin world at least, and fixing on a rock for their "Golgothana rupes" . . . that they should have arranged the other localities with reference to it as they found them set down in the plan.'

It is scarcely necessary to say much with regard to an argument so ingenious and unpractical. Canon Williams very justly observes that the whole assumption is overthrown by the simple fact that the church of the eleventh century was built by the Greeks, and not by the Latins.

It is quite impossible to suppose, without reason, that in the eleventh century the Christians, whether Latins or Greeks, wishing to build on the present site of the Holy Sepulchre a church similar in plan to that of the Dome of the Rock, should have had recourse to the plan of Arculf, instead of getting the plan from the Dome itself.

It is also quite impossible to believe that Arculf's plan can be taken from the Dome of the Rock.

I contrast the plan of Arculf with the plan of the Dome :

ARCULF'S PLAN AND ACCOUNT.	DOME OF THE ROCK.
1. A round building, with four entrances to north-east and south-east, like the present building over the Holy Sepulchre.	1. An octagonal building with doors to four cardinal points of the compass.
2. Door of the cave to *east* as in the present Holy Sepulchre.	2. Door of the cave to the *south-east*.
3. Place where the body was laid, on the north side of the *inner* chamber, as at present, on a bench.	3. No *inner* chamber, and no bench.
4. Nine men could stand in the cave, as at present.	4. One hundred men could stand in the cave.
5. There were three altars to the north, south, and west, and to the present day the niches for these altars remain.	5. Not a sign of these, or any place where such altars can have been placed.
6. The Dome was supported by twelve stone columns of extraordinary magnitude. (See plan of the present Holy Sepulchre.)	6. Account not applicable to the present Dome of the Rock.
7. The exterior of the sepulchre was covered with choice marble to the top of the roof.	7. A statement not applicable to the Sakhra, which only rises about five feet above the floor-level.
8. Several other churches are described very similar in plan to those now existing at the Holy Sepulchre.	8. Not a vestige of any buildings now to be seen around the Dome of the Rock, except the small Dome.

It would be interesting if Mr. Fergusson would elaborate a hypothetical restoration of the Dome of the Rock buildings in the time of Arculf. It is significant that he does not attempt to explain how it is that the plan of Arculf should be entirely unlike the octagonal plan of the Dome of the Rock.

47. [H. S., p. 55.] 'Two or three centuries after the capture of the city, the Saracens had increased in power relatively to the Christians, while the capitulation of Omar had fallen into desuetude, and *the Moslems then cast longing eyes on the Dome of the Rock;* either because they were offended that the Christians should possess a more splendid building than themselves in the immediate proximity of and in front of their Aksa, or it may have been *that they coveted the custody of the Tomb of Christ, whom they look upon as the greatest of prophets next to Mahomet.'*

[Page 73.] 'When we recollect how fervently the Moslems reverence the Tombs of Abraham, Isaac, and Jacob, at Hebron, and how sacredly they have guarded the Tomb of St. John at Damascus, and how rigidly they have excluded Christians from visiting it, we should not be surprised at their *desire to possess the Tomb of Christ*, whom they look upon as only second to Mahomet, nor that they should since have prevented His disciples from gaining access to its sacred precincts.'

['Bib. Dic.,' Smith, p. 1029.] 'Fortunately, however, the Moslems *respected the Tomb of Christ*, whom they consider one of the seven prophets, inferior only to the founder of their religion, and they left the Dome of the Rock uninjured as we now see it.'

[H. S., p. 129.] 'There is absolutely no hint in any author, Christian or Mahometan, that I know of, that the Moslems either burnt or destroyed the Anastasis, or Tomb of Christ. To have done so would have been considered as great a sacrilege by the Mahometans as by the Christians.'

Remarks.—It is difficult to realise that Mr. Fergusson

can be so unversed in the views entertained by the Moslems concerning the Tomb of Christ, as he would appear to be from the perusal of these extracts. Is the following a proof of the reverence he asserts they have for the Holy Sepulchre?

'The Moslems changed the name of the Great Christian Church from Caiyameh (Anastasis) to Camamah (dung), to remind them of their indecent treatment of the Holy Place, and to further glorify the Sakhra itself.'—Besant and Palmer, p. 77.

'Verily, Jesus Christ, the son of Mary, is the Apostle of God. . . . Yet Jesus was a mere mortal; and at the Day of Judgment his testimony will serve to condemn both the Jews, who reject him, and the Christians who adore him as the Son of God. . . . The malice of his enemies aspersed his reputation, and conspired against his life; but their intention only was guilty: a phantom or a criminal was substituted on the cross, and the innocent saint was translated to the seventh heaven.'—Gibbon, vol. v. ch. 50.

What possible reverence could the Moslems have for a tomb which never received the body of their prophet Isa, and which received in its place that of a criminal?

Mr. Fergusson is not aware of, or has lost sight of, the fact that while they honour their prophet Isa they can have no feelings save those of repulsion regarding a tomb in which Isa had not been laid: for, according to their view, Isa was caught up in the air from Gethsemane.

'Go ye not to the Church of Mary in the Holy House, or to the Church of the Body of Christ, or to the Two Pillars in the Church of Mount Olivet; for these are all of them idolatrous.'—Jalal-ed-din, p. 142.

Author's note to ditto : ' The Moslems imagine that our Lord did not Himself suffer, but was caught up to heaven : Judas being substituted and crucified in His room. They therefore disregard all places connected with His crucifixion, burial, and resurrection.'

The Church of the Holy Sepulchre is therefore to the Moslems the Tomb of Judas the criminal.

48. [H. S., p. 71, note.] 'A curious instance of the respect in which the Mohametans, *after the Crusades*, *held the Christian localities*, occurs in the travels of Ricoldus de Monte Crucis, who visited Jerusalem about the end of the thirteenth century. Describing the valley of Jehoshaphat, he adds : ' Inde intravimus in sepulchrum pulcherrimum Virginis quod Saraceni cum multis liminaribus, et magnâ reverentiâ custodiunt.'

Remarks.—Another erroneous view. Mr. Fergusson, in order that he may show more fully that the Moslems revered the Tomb of Christ, now essays to prove that after the Crusades they held in reverence other Christian localities, notably the Tomb of the Blessed Virgin in the Kidron Valley. In the first place it was not after the Crusades, but from the establishment of their religion that they revered this tomb in the Kidron, as will be shown by quotations from one of those authorities which Mr. Fergusson considers most reliable, viz., Jalal-ed-din.

In the second place, the Tomb of Sitti Maryam is not to the Moslem merely a Christian locality. It is one of those numerous places attractive to both Christians and Moslems. But the Moslems look at these places through their own eyes, not through ours. To the Moslems the Sitti Maryam (Our Lady the Virgin) is no more or less a Christian saint than to us she is a Moslem saint. A Moslem author might, with equal justness, object to Mr. Fergusson worshipping at the Tomb of the Sitti Maryam, because she is a Moslem saint. This is most clear and indubitable, and to point it out I will commence with a reference to Abraham, which will indicate the line of thought of the Moslems.

'Abraham was neither Jew nor Christian, but an orthodox Moslem.'—Jalal-ed-din, ch. xi.

'It is said that three women have been prophetesses, viz. Sarah, and the mother of Moses, and Maria, daughter of Imram: for Sarah received by revelation the joyful news of the birth of Isaac; Moses' birth was divinely communicated to his mother; and Maria received from an angel the happy tidings of the birth of Jesus.'—Ibid., ch. xii.

'Go ye not into the Church of Maria in the Holy House, or to the Church of the Body of Christ, or to the Two Pillars in the Church of Mount Olivet; for these are all of them idolatrous. . . . *All is inefficacious* which they have built, except the church in the Valley of Gehenna.'—Ibid., ch. ix.

'When Omar conquered Jerusalem, he passed by the Church of Mary, situated in the valley, and offered there two prayers; he afterwards repented, remembering the word of the prophet, who said that this valley is one of the valleys of Gehinnum.'—Merj-ed-din.

It is thus clear that the Tomb of Sitti Maryam is the shrine of a Moslem prophetess, although at the same time to the Christians it is also a point of attraction; and it is shown that Mr. Fergusson has no case in his endeavour to prove that the Moslems wished to usurp the Tomb of Christ—that is to say if Merj-ed-din and Jalal-ed-din are to be credited, and Mr. Fergusson has stated they are most deserving of credit.

49. [H. S., p. 57.] 'The exact epoch when the transference took place is more difficult to fix than the mode, but fortunately it is of infinitely less consequence. To take a familiar illustration. Suppose in 1850 you found a certain Mr. Smith carrying on business and living over his shop in Oxford Street, and in 1860 found the same person settled for like purposes in the Strand: you would feel certain that between those dates a transference had taken place.'

Remarks.—Mr. Fergusson was apparently more certain about the date of this mythical transference when he published an essay in 1847, for he then said (p. 164) that the Christians were forced to abandon the Dome of the Rock in A.D. 969, and built another Holy Sepulchre on the present site about A. D. 1031, and that the only objection to his proposition was its improbability.

Mr. Fergusson, after thirty-four years' consideration and reflection, still finds the theory of a transference so improbable that he cannot even now suggest a date when it could have taken place nearer than 'from the time of Charlemagne to that of the Crusades.'

His illustration regarding the transference with reference to Mr. Smith's shop is not by any means a parallel case.

50. [' Bib. Dic.,' Smith, p. 1032.] 'Nothing, however, can be more remarkable than the different ways in which the Crusaders treated the Dome of the Rock and Mosque el Aksa; the latter they always called the " Templum seu palatium Solomonis," and treated it with the contempt always applied by Christians to anything Jewish. The mosque was turned into a stable, the buildings into dwellings for knights, who took the title of Knights Templars, from their residence in the Temple. But the Dome of the Rock they called " Templum Domini."

'Priests and choir were appointed to perform service in it, and during the whole time of the Christian occupation it was held certainly as sacred, if not more so, than the Church of the Holy Sepulchre in the town. Had they believed or suspected that the rock was that on which the Jewish Temple stood, it would have been treated as the Aksa was; but they knew that the Dome of the Rock was a Christian building and sacred to the Saviour, though in the uncritical spirit of the age they never seem exactly to have known either what it was or by whom it was erected.'

['Essay,' p. 181.] 'One other very curious fact is mentioned by this author [Sæwulf], which is the print of the foot of Christ left on the rock when He escaped from the Temple, lest the Jews should stone Him. I have very little doubt indeed that this was originally the print supposed to be left when He rose from the tomb. It now is understood to be that of Mahomet, when he ascended to heaven from this rock on the celebrated night journey, and is held in the greatest reverence by his followers.'

[Page 13.] 'Sæwulf was an ignorant savage, who believed whatever he was told, and was incapable of forming an independent judgment.'

[Page 185.] 'And immediately on the recovery of the city by the Crusaders, they adopted this church as the principal one of Jerusalem, *after the Holy Sepulchre*, and with the Mahometan tradition, that the rock in its centre was the Holy of Holies of the cursed Temple of the ten times accursed Jews.'

Remarks.—Mr. Fergusson again takes a highly ingenious line of argument, and quotes in his support Sæwulf, whom he afterwards stigmatises as an ignorant savage. He argues that the Christians of the time of the Crusaders hated the site of the Jewish Temple, and that therefore they used it as a palace for their knights, while they revered the Dome of the Rock as the Sepulchre of our Lord. He appears to have forgotten that this would have taken place after his supposed transference, and when it is certain that the present Holy Sepulchre was in existence even by his own admission. At this time there was intense squabbling between the Greeks and Latins, secular and regular. If the Knights Templars had the slightest conception of Mr. Fergusson's theory (as he asserts they had), would they not have advocated as strenuously as Mr. Fergusson that the Dome of the Rock was the Holy Sepulchre? Is there a doubt that they would have asserted this mythical rival claim, in their hatred of the Patriarch of Jerusalem and his party.

Mr. Fergusson is quite in error in stating that the Knights of the Temple treated the Temple, after which they were called, with contempt: they revered the site, more particularly because it was rendered the more sacred by the frequent visits and footsteps of our Lord. Jalal-ed-din states, in speaking of the occupation of the Dome of the Rock by the Crusaders, that they had built a little chapel over the Sakhra, and said, 'This was the place whereon Christ set His foot.'

Mr. Fergusson also is entirely confused about the terms 'Templum Domini,' 'Templum Solomonis,' 'Porticus Solomonis,' and 'Palatium Solomonis.' The solution of his difficulty is very simple. 'Templum Domini' is not 'the Temple of *our* Lord,' but 'the Temple of *the* Lord;' that is to say, it has nothing to do with the Holy Sepulchre, but is the Dome of the Rock, the site of the Jewish Temple. 'Porticus Solomonis' is Solomon's Porch, on the east wall running up to the Golden Gate; and 'Palatium seu Templum Solomonis' is the site of Solomon's Palace and adjacent buildings of the Court of the Gentiles, added on by King Herod, and not forming part of the original Temple: this was occupied by the Knights Templars. There was nothing accursed to the Latin Christians about the site of the Temple that I can discover; if there were, would the term ' Templars' have been a title of honour?

51. [H. S., p. 47.] 'If we apply these words, or indeed any expression of Eusebius, to the present buildings, there is nothing which can be made in any way applicable. Its defenders are obliged to have recourse to fire and destructions to obtain even a negative accordance of the text with the existing buildings; but even this will not get over the indication of the locality being opposite to the old Jerusalem ' (No. 1).

[Page 50.] 'The next great event in the history of the sacred localities is the capture of the city by the Persians in A.D. 614, and the reported destruction of the Christian churches by fire at that time. This fire has been as useful to the advocates of the present localities as that at Wolf's Crag was to Caleb Balderston, though it would be easy to show that the damage done by the Persians was about equal to that effected by the Scotch conflagration. In the first place, Eutychius, who is the principal authority in this case, expressly says that two only of the churches were damaged by fire, ' igne injecto;' in two others only plundered. But the great proof is that a simple monk, named Modestus, restored the whole to their pristine magnificence, without means, or money, at a time when the city was still at the mercy of the Persians, and its wretched inhabitants subsisting on the alms of the Egyptian patriarch. And we find no further complaint of the damage done by the Persians either at the Mahometan conquest, twenty-three years afterwards, or when Arculfus describes the four churches as complete and perfect at the end of the same century in which the Persian invasion took place.'

Remarks.—History entirely refutes Mr. Fergusson in this assertion, as has already been shown. 'In the month of June, 614, the Holy City was invested and taken by storm . . . the splendid churches were thrown down, and that of the Holy Sepulchre burnt with fire.'—Robinson, i. sec. viii.

'The Sepulchre of Christ, and the stately churches of Helena and Constantine were consumed, or at least damaged, by the flames.'—Gibbon, v. ch. xlvi.

'Then the Basilica of Constantine, the Churches of Calvary and of the Holy Sepulchre, were demolished; the last two being burnt to the ground.'—Williams, i. ch. iv.

'Every Christian church was demolished, that of the Holy Sepulchre was the great object of furious hatred; the stately building of Helena and Constantine was abandoned to the flames.'—Milman, b. xxi.

When it is considerd that the attacking party was composed of Magi and Jews, hating the Christians, it is reasonable to suppose that Dr. Milman is strictly correct in his statement that the Church of the Holy Sepulchre was completely destroyed.

The rebuilding of the church by Modestus is equally a matter of history: the funds being principally supplied by the Patriarch of Alexandria, the amount of which is enumerated by Williams (i. ch. iv.).

There were other partial destructions of the Holy Places, but that by the mad Hakim was most complete. For reasons best known to himself this latter destruction does not appear to be prominently mentioned by Mr. Fergusson in his work on the 'Holy Sepulchre.'

'The Temple of the Christian world, the Church of the Resurrection, was demolished to its foundations.' —Gibbon, vi. ch. lvii.

'The luminous prodigy of Easter was interrupted, and much profane labour exhausted to destroy the cave in the rock, which properly constituted the Holy Sepulchre, A.D. 1010.'

Mr. Fergusson himself says ('Essay,' p. 176), 'All the historians of that age narrate the total destruction of the Holy Sepulchre by the Kalif Hakim, A.D. 1010.'

52. [H. S., p. 129.] 'El Hakim did burn and destroy the Basilica of Constantine, sometimes called the Church of the Holy Sepulchre, and no trace of it is left, except in the Golden Gateway ; but there is no hint in any author, Christian or Mahometan, that I know of, that the Moslems either burnt or destroyed the Anastasis, or Tomb of Christ. To have done so would have been considered nearly as great sacrilege of the Mahometans as by the Christians.'

Remarks.—Mr. Fergusson is again at issue with all historians. Gibbon's account that even the rock itself was attacked is most clear and explicit. Glabu and Ademar are the authorities for this. The order given by Hakim was as follows : 'The Imâm commands you to destroy the Temple of the Resurrection, so that its heaven may become earth, and its length may become breadth.'—De Lacy.

Hakim, his followers, and the Moslems generally, could have no reverence whatever for the Anastasis, as has already been shown (No. 46).

53. [H. S., p. 9.] 'The reiterated assertion of Theodoricus that that building [the Dome of the Rock] was erected by Constantine and his mother Helena, as Dr. Tobler says, "takes the first blush of novelty off Mr. Fergusson's theory," though in a manner which may be considered most satisfactory.'

Remarks.—Theodoricus is supposed to have written A.D. 1178, and his statement as to the Dome of the Rock having been built by Helena is no evidence either way. It is a remark he would probably have made of any church of consequence. 'In the writings and traditions of succeeding centuries, the name of Helena became more prominent. Her memory and her deeds were emblazoned and magnified in story as successive ages rolled on, until, in the fourteenth century, not less than thirty churches were ascribed to her within the limits of Palestine; and to the present day almost every remaining church of that country of any antiquity is in like manner referred in monastic tradition to the munificence of Helena.'— Robinson, i. sec. viii.

Gibbon, in a note to chapter lix., says, 'The clergy artfully confounded the Mosch, or Church of the Temple, with the Holy Sepulchre, and their wilful error has deceived Vertot and Muratori.'

54. ['Essay,' p. 107.] 'So far as the Mahometans are concerned, they never in any age or any country erected a building with a ceiled roof, of this or indeed of any other sort ; certainly, so far as my knowledge extends, in no single instance.'

Remarks.—Mr. Fergusson, in the previous sentence (p. 107), had asserted that the present ceilings in the Dome of the Rock are those erected by Constantine. This proposition has already been justly scouted by Canon Williams, and it is too ridiculous (from Mr. Fergusson's point of view) to be treated seriously, for Mr. Fergusson himself admits the historical truth of the several conflagrations to which the Holy Sepulchre was subjected.

But there is another assertion quite as startling, viz., that '*the Mahometans never in any age or in any country erected a building with a ceiled roof, of this or indeed of any other sort*'!

This is enough to settle Mr. Fergusson's pretensions to be an exponent of Moslem architecture. If he were to travel through Syria, Northern Africa, and Spain, he would be able to acquire some better knowledge of the ceiled roofs erected by the Moslems in various ages, and would be the better enabled to judge whether the ceilings of the Dome of the Rock are Moslem or not.

55. ['Essay,' p. 122.] 'I am particular in pointing out this irregularity in the vaults [S. E. angle of Haram] because, though it would appear of very small importance to most people, to me it is almost proof positive that Justinian's church was situated over them, or in a continuation of them. The subject is so familiar to my mind as scarcely to require pointing out; but I question if, even after I explain myself, many will follow me. It is this, that the widest of the central vaults (30 feet) is to the two on each side of it (21 feet) in the ratio of the square to the hypothenuse of an equilateral triangle to the square of its sides; or to be less mathematical, if four of the sides of an octagon are produced till they form a square, as in the annexed diagram, each side of that square will be divided into three parts, of which the centre one will be to those on each side of it in the ratio of 10 to 7 nearly, or as 30 to 21: and I cannot conceive they should have been so spaced unless it was to receive an octagon roof.'

Remarks.—This 'proof positive' or 'damning testimony' is considerably injured by the fact that the vaults are not spaced as Mr. Fergusson states. On reference to the Ordnance Survey it will be seen that the central vault measures about 29 feet from centre to centre of pier, the vault to the south, 18 feet, and that to the north 25 feet from centre to centre. Thus the supposed dimensions of 21, 30, 31, are really represented by 25, 29, 18. It would be interesting to ascertain what fresh coincidence Mr. Fergusson will discover with these amended figures.

A very good reason may be assigned for the extra width of this centre vault. The single gate opens into it, and below is the very curious chamber built under the level of the vaults, which is supposed to be the passage for the blood : the building of the vaults above probably depended in the spacing of the substructures below.

In 'The Temples of the Jews,' Mr. Fergusson forgets conveniently all about his proof positive, and places his church of Justinian again in a different position.

56. [H. S., p. 72.] 'Notwithstanding the evidence of the Cufic character of the writing, I cannot help fancying the whole is of the time of Saladin. But this is a point regarding which others are more competent to judge than I am.'

[Page ix.] 'The second, giving the inscriptions on the Dome of the Rock as they existed A.D. 1172, renders it nearly certain that the Arabic inscriptions which now adorn the building are as late as Saladin's time, as suggested in the text.'

['Essay,' p. 181.] 'The only author that takes a view distinctly opposed to this, that I am aware of, is William of Tyre, and he asserts twice over that it was built by Omar Ibn Khatah, and appeals to the inscriptions on its walls as testimony of this, but with an earnestness that looks very suspicious : and I cannot help thinking, that as Archbishop of Tyre he was in the secret, and consequently anxious to conceal it.'

Remarks.—Professor Palmer, the eminent Arabic scholar, states, 'It must be distinctly understood that Arabic historians are as clear and explicit as to the building of the splendid Dome as we should be on the building of St. Paul's by Christopher Wren.'

It has been stated that where poisonous plants grow, not far off may be found the antidotes: so with Mr. Fergusson's writings regarding Jerusalem; wherever he makes a remarkable statement, not far off may be found a contradiction totally annihilating its force in the hands of those who know how to use it. He is most strenuous as to certain architectural details giving the age of buildings, and yet he must have a different rule for caligraphy, and would have us believe that the Cufic writing of the seventh century extended so far down, without alteration, to the thirteenth or fourteenth century; however, he entertained different views in 1847, when the shape of the letters did not appear to tell against his theory: 'And though they probably contain sentences from the Koran, *the form of the letters would be almost as certain a guide to their age as the details of the architecture.*'—'Essay,' p. 115.

Now, however, that the form of the letters tells against Mr. Fergusson's theory, the subject has another aspect to him.

Poor William of Tyre, how has he offended Mr. Fergusson? Why should his earnestness be suspicious, merely because he presumes to differ from Mr. Fergusson? And why should the statements of the unknown

Theodoricus and the phantom Innominatus be allowed to destroy the 'damning testimonies' of known historians, simply because their writings can be twisted to favour Mr. Fergusson's theory in some respects?

The statement of Theodoricus does not, however, really affect the question: it is evident that eight of the inscriptions he alludes to were on the eight sides of the building. Whether the long Latin inscription he cites was above, below, or painted over the mosaics of the Cufic inscription is not stated, but there is certainly no reason for supposing that the Cufic inscription did not exist at the same time as those in Latin.

Professor Palmer states: 'The only inscription of Abd-el-Melek which now remains in the Mosque [Dome of the Rock] is the great mosaic around the colonnade in the interior; its preservation during the subsequent Christian occupation of the city may occasion some surprise, as the Latins (by whom the Cubbeh es Sakhra was turned into a church) could not but have been offended at quotations which so decidedly deny the divinity of Christ and the doctrine of the Trinity. It is probable, however, that the Cufic character, in which it is written, was as intelligible to the Christian natives of that time, as it is now even to most of the learned Moslems of the present day.'

57. ['The Temples of the Jews.' p. 74.] 'Between these two points we have a perfectly level area, measuring about 600 feet each way.'

Remarks.—In actual practice Mr. Fergusson is obliged to put up with a levelled space of made ground hanging over the bottom of the Tyropœon valley, 585 feet by 610 feet. This is somewhat of a poor result to arrive at after discarding so many of the measurements of Josephus for the purpose of keeping the Temple to 600 feet per side.

['The Temples of the Jews,' p. 17.] 'On the Survey, however, the distance measures only 585 feet, English.'

Remarks.—So that after all Mr. Fergusson's re-iterations that his hypothetical temple fits in between the west wall of the Haram and the Double Gate, he allows himself that he has only 585 feet for a length of $607\frac{1}{2}$ feet. And somehow or other, upon this basis, he arrives at the conclusion that the cubit measured 18 English inches, and not 18 Greek inches.

58. ['The Temples of the Jews,' p. 11, Note 1.] 'The praise of accuracy must be understood as applying only to the work of Major Wilson, which was engraved at the Ordnance Office at Southampton. The surveys of Captain Warren, though equally executed by sappers, have only been published in rough lithographs executed from tentative drawings sent home by him during the progress of the Survey, or in a popular manner, and on a small scale, in a work entitled "The Recovery of Jerusalem in 1860." As neither of them make any pretension to scientific accuracy, Major Wilson has undertaken to republish his notes, incorporating Captain Warren's work with his own. The difficulty, however, of reconciling the

two has been so great, the task has been indefinitely delayed, and may not improbably have to be abandoned. We know roughly the result of Captain Warren's three years' exploration, but in a form which, to say the least of it, is extremely unsatisfatory, and which can in no instance be implicitly relied upon.'

['The Temples of the Jews,' p. 172, Note 1.] 'Major Wilson informs me that he has found it impossible to protract Captain Warren's data in such a manner as to make them agree with the Ordnance Survey. The explanation of the discrepancy, as I understand it, is that Captain Warren only jotted down in a hurried manner, his discoveries as he made them, intending to go over the whole with the sappers, when they were complete, and make a careful survey of them. On his return from Jericho, however, he found the vaults closed by order of the Pacha, and he was never able afterwards to gain access to them.'

Remarks.—These notes by Mr. Fergusson are examples of his extraordinary power of (what I may term) writing epigrams of errors and misstatements, the tendency of which are evident. Colonel Wilson agrees with Mr. Fergusson, and therefore all his work must be accurate. I disagree with Mr. Fergusson, and therefore all my work is in error.

Mr. Ferguson would imply that Colonel Wilson has given him this impression regarding my work which he now, on Colonel Wilson's authority, endeavours to convey to the public ; I will show that this is not so, and that Mr. Fergusson, in endeavouring to injure my reputation for accuracy in taking measurements, has involved himself in some very peculiar difficulties. In the first place, the Ordnance Survey of Jerusalem, executed by men from the Ordnance Survey, and generally superintended by Colonel Wilson, was the superficial measurement of the ground, while my work was in a great measure confined to measurement of works underground; and generally speaking, it may be said that while the Ordnance Survey made the plans of the walls of Jerusalem, I made the elevations. It is obvious, therefore, that in itself the charge of not being able to reconcile the two is somewhat difficult to understand ; but if it were correct, it is an assumption on Mr. Fergusson's part that I must be wrong, and that the Ordnance Survey must be right. As a matter of fact there were exceedingly few discrepancies met with, certainly not more than are usually met with in comparing so-called accurate pieces of work ; and when they did occur, I think it can be shown that my measurements were correct.

The inference that Mr. Fergusson would endeavour to draw, viz., that rough lithographs are less accurate in themselves than copperplate engraving, is scarcely applicable or to the point. *Cæteris paribus*, there is no doubt that the former are more accurate than the latter ; but a faithful lithograph can scarcely make an accurate drawing inaccurate, neither can a copperplate make an inaccurate drawing accurate, and the question, so far as the relative accuracy of my work and that of the Ordnance Survey, must be judged before the work is engraved. It could make no difference to my measurements whether the Palestine Exploration Fund chose to publish my work on rough lithographs, as Mr. Fergusson asserts they have done, or on copperplate, as was done by the Ordnance Survey: therefore Mr. Fergusson's strictures so far, if of any value at all, are really levelled against the Palestine Exploration Fund (of which he is one of the General Committee, and a leading and influential member) for not having had my drawings more carefully engraved.

The statement by Mr. Fergusson that the work of the Ordnance Survey and myself could not be reconciled, and that therefore the task of incorporating my work with Colonel Wilson's will have to be abandoned, is most completely contradicted by Colonel Wilson himself, who says:

'The notes on the Haram wall were written two or three years ago as part of a revised edition of the notes to the "Ordnance Survey of Jerusalem." I was obliged, from pressure of other work, to lay the notes on one side, and have never been able to continue them. I have offered the notes as a contribution to the "Quarterly Statement," hoping that they may be found useful in future discussions respecting the character of the masonry of the Haram wall.'

'The plan I adopted in the notes was to give, in the first place, a description of each section of the wall from the "Recovery of Jerusalem," the "Quarterly Statements," and other sources, and then to add such remarks as occurred to me; the facts are thus separated from the comments.'

'It was my intention to embody in the new edition of the "Ordnance Survey Notes" a description of the excavations made by Captain, now Lieut.-Colonel, Warren at Jerusalem. The nature of those excavations, and the difficulties which Colonel Warren encountered and successfully overcame, have never been sufficiently appreciated by the public. Though I cannot always agree with the conclusions which he has drawn from the results of the excavations, I am glad to take this opportunity of expressing my sense of the great value and importance of his work at Jerusalem.'

But it is still more completely contradicted by the fact that my work was incorporated with the Ordnance Survey plates in 1876, of which Mr. Fergusson was aware, for he actually quotes from a remark of mine on the revised Ordnance Survey plan, and puts in a footnote 'Last edition of Ordnance Survey map, 1876' (*vide* 'Temples of the Jews,' p. 236). Thus we have in one portion of his work, Mr. Fergusson stating that for want of reconciliation my work cannot be plotted on the Ordnance Survey plans; and in another portion, we find Mr. Fergusson actually quoting from the revised plans, on which are embodied my work. Surely, at the least, Mr. Fergusson is very much wanting in accuracy when he makes such contradictory statements. The facts regarding the embodiment of my work on the Ordnance Survey plates are as follows. For some years past Colonel Wilson had wished to revise the Ordnance Survey notes and plates, which had got quite out of date, owing to the excavations at Jerusalem, and considered that my work should be added on to the plates thus revised. In this I quite concurred, and was ready to give my assistance, more particularly as the Palestine Exploration Fund could not afford to publish expensive plates showing my work, and because there is no doubt that, apart from other considerations, the Ordnance Survey plates should be kept up to date.

I therefore readily consented to assist Major Wilson, when on the 1st May, 1876, he wrote to me, stating that after a long correspondence with the Treasury, they had consented to bring out 'revised plans of Jerusalem,' and a new edition of the 'Notes' in an octavo form, and further asked me to help him in the supervision of the drawing of the maps.

Accordingly the whole of the additions to the revised Ordnance Survey plates, which were ready before I left for South Africa in October 1876, were subject to my direct supervision, so far as they had to do with the excavations, the draftsman employed having simply to copy my drawings on the same scale. I had myself carefully drawn in all the additions to the general plan, $\frac{1}{500}$ on the Ordnance Survey plates, so that this work had simply to be transferred from mine. There are a few points, however, which have been added, and in which I do not agree; for example, the Ordnance Survey plate of the section of the Haram Wall at Bab al Mugharibe, shows the rock running to east as a precipice, whereas all local indications point out that it actually rises very gently; the placing of this precipitous rock here is in accordance with a proposal of Mr. Fergusson, who wants it there for his Temple to rest on. The revised plans of the Ordnance Survey showing my work are stated to have been *prepared* by Colonel Wilson: I have requested the Committee of the Palestine Exploration Fund to examine them, and to give an opinion whether they are my plans or not. I should like to hear Colonel Wilson's account of what he actually said to Mr. Fergusson regarding the plotting of my work. There is the one case where I found that the plotting of the work about the secret passages, west of Wilson's Arch, did not agree with the streets above; but it is first necessary to know that they should agree, and if they should, it is quite as probable that the Ordnance Survey is wrong as that I am. I have written to Jerusalem to have some measurements taken. The fact, however, that there was one discrepancy between the direction of a tunnel underground and a street above ground, is certainly not any handle for the sweeping assertion of Mr. Fergusson that my work cannot be reconciled with the Ordnance Survey, neither is it any argument whatever that I must be wrong even in this single point, although I am too experienced a surveyor to believe myself to be infallible. The statement of Mr. Fergusson that my work 'can in no instance be implicitly relied on,' is absolutely without foundation, unless he means it as an observation applicable to all classes of work. I readily acknowledge that rigid accuracy cannot be attained, but Mr. Fergusson must be well aware that my measurements are well known to be 'strictly accurate;' and the proof of this is that he has not yet been able to show me in error, while I have but to point out error after error in his statements about Jerusalem.

I will now mention a matter which will read almost ludicrously after his stricture upon me.

When I was at Jerusalem, I corrected several errors in the Ordnance Survey plans, and among others found that the great cistern, the 'bath-house' of the Temple (*vide* Plate V., the 'Temples of the Jews'), was about fifty feet too far to the north of its true position. This has accordingly been rectified by Colonel Wilson in the revised plates issued in 1876, which Mr. Fergusson has examined (even if he has not them in his possession); and yet while accusing me of inaccuracy, Mr. Fergusson actually issues in 1878 a plan, purporting to be a reduction from the Ordnance Survey, with this error still shown on it.

On reference to the plate it will be seen that he places this tank over the Kubbat al Arwah, instead of some fifty feet farther south, where its prolongation would strike the steps next to his '*Possible Extension*.' This is somewhat turning the tables on Mr. Fergusson. He charges me with inaccuracy, states that my work cannot be reconciled with that of the Ordnance Survey, and that, therefore, the revision of the Ordnance Survey plates will probably have to be abandoned: and I show that he can prove no inaccuracy in my work; that when inaccuracies are apparent, they are known to be in the Ordnance Survey work; that the Ordnance Survey plates *have* been revised two years before his book was written; that Mr. Fergusson knew them to have been so revised, and had seen them (for he quotes from them), and that the revision of the parts affecting my work was done from my drawings and subject to my inspection; and moreover that Mr. Fergusson actually gives in 1878 an incorrect plan of the Haram area, which had been correctly revised under my inspection since 1876, and yet talks about accuracy in a manner that would lead the public to depend upon his plans, and consider mine inaccurate. But I have not yet quite taken leave of Mr. Fergusson in this matter.

I should be glad to know, and I am sure the public would also, especially practical builders who might find the knowledge of the process of use to them—I should like to know if Mr. Fergusson seriously intends us to believe (among his other curious proposals) that the Dome of the Mosque has actually turned round nearly three degrees upon its centre since it was built; and if so, how he accounts for this remarkable movement of a building, and how the movement was accomplished.

If Mr. Fergusson states that it has not moved, then I ask why he shows it in a different position in the Haram area in Plate V. (A.D. 1878) to that in which it is shown in Plate VII. (A.D. 333); an alteration, by the way, which would materially strengthen his argument, if it could be permitted.

On the other hand, if Mr. Fergusson states that he has not drawn this alteration in himself, and has not given his draftsman instructions to do so, I say here is an instance in Mr. Fergusson's drawing of a very serious misrepresentation of the position of an existing building, which materially strengthens his views, and which he has neglected to correct. Surely after this Mr. Fergusson should be careful how he imputes want of accuracy in others.

In order more fully to explain this matter, I must enter somewhat into details.

A few days ago I was examining the Ordnance Survey plan of the Noble Sanctuary, and was noting down the old line of buildings which are parallel to the east wall, and those which are, respectively, parallel to and perpendicular to the west and south walls. I then found that the northern portion of the Dome of the Rock platform (on which Mr. Fergusson places the Basilica of Constantine), and also a portion of the sacred rock itself, and many other portions of the northern part of the Sanctuary, can be referred as parallel to the east wall, while in the southern portion the Aksa Mosque and adjoining building can be referred in the same way to the south and west walls.

I then reasoned as a test regarding the building of the Dome of the Rock: 'If it were built by Abd al Melek as part of the Masjid el Aksa, it should be built with reference to the Aksa Mosque and the west wall of the Sanctuary; while if (according to Mr. Fergusson) it was built by Constantine, it should be referable to the east wall of the Sanctuary, and be parallel to the Golden Gate and northern side of the platform, where he places the Basilica of Constantine.'

I find, on examination, that it is referable to the Aksa and west wall, and not to the Golden Gate and east wall.

This is one of those cases of unconscious testimony, which Mr. Fergusson calls 'damning evidences,' which so strongly tell against his theory. And I then turned to his Plate VII., where he has grouped together his various hypothetical buildings according to dates, as I wanted to see how he got over the fact that the Dome of the Rock is not built in conformity with the lines of the buildings he has grouped around it.

To my amazement I discovered, on looking at Plate VII., that Mr. Fergusson had actually turned the Dome of the Rock round on its centre so as to be referable to the east wall instead of the west wall.

59. ['The Temples of the Jews,' p. 15, Note 2.] 'Captain Warren not only uses the large cubit, but assumes that, when Josephus said feet—which, by the way, he never did, in so far as the plans are concerned —he meant cubits, and on these two assumptions he bases his restoration of the Temple.'

[Page 15.] 'The only exception to this is where Josephus, with his usual tendency to exaggerate, uses cubits, when the real dimension is only the same number of feet; as, for instance, in describing the altar, he says it was 50 cubits square, and 15 cubits in height, whereas we shall see in the sequel it was 33 cubits, or 49½ feet across, and 10 cubits or 15 feet in height.'

There is something ludicrous in such direct contradictions placed together on one page. In the first place he calls me to account for supposing that Josephus may have meant cubits when he said feet, and then in the same breath himself states, that when Josephus meant feet he said cubits. Mr. Fergusson does not explain his reasons for keeping me within such bounds while he allows himself such latitude.

60. ['The Temples of the Jews,' p. 41.] 'Herod certainly built nothing in this angle' (S. E. angle of Haram area).

[Ibid., p. 246.] 'That the palace was burnt when the city was taken is more than probable; but even supposing it was not rebuilt and occupied as a palace after the return, it is most improbable that so valuable a site would have been allowed to lie waste or covered with ruins. *It must have been utilised in some way or other.*'

Remarks.—Here Mr. Fergusson is in another difficulty. He has at last accepted my proposal that the south-eastern angle of the Noble Sanctuary is the site of Solomon's palace. He supposes that it was burnt at the capture of Jerusalem, and that after the return from the captivity it was so valuable a site that it must have been utilised, and even after Herod's time he asserts that here Justinian built his Mary Church; and yet he denies that Herod built here or utilised this site. Then must I ask, what was done with the site during Herod's time—was it left as a charred and smouldering ruin adjoining the Temple? That it was there is manifest, because it existed in Solomon's time and exists now; the south-eastern angle still standing erect and *in situ*. Mr. Fergusson cannot solve this question. I solve it by showing that Herod brought this building into the area of the Temple.

61. ['The Temples of the Jews,' p. 36]. 'In his own woodcut plan, which is a reduction from the Ordnance Survey, the rock rises to the surface between the contours 2419, 2429, while his 2410 in the annexed plan passes at least ten feet below it, and the same mistake occurs where the rock rises to the surface near the Golden Gate.'

[Ibid., p. 37.] 'Warren's contour, 4310 (4320, it ought to be).'

Remarks.—This is another of Mr. Fergusson's remarkable statements. I can only say that he is completely in error in this matter, and that my contour 4310 should not be 4320, as stated by him. Lieut. Conder agrees with me in this.—*Vide* 'Quarterly Statement,' p. 9, January, 1880.

62. ['The Temples of the Jews,' p. 166.] 'The reading of the Law, the putting up of prayer, the chanting of the psalms, if these took place at all except in the open air, must, as before suggested, have taken place in the upper room of the Temple.'

Remarks.—Here Mr. Fergusson, in order to prove

that there was an Alijah or upper chamber in Herod's Temple, suggests that the service was conducted there when not in the open air. It is needless to reply to such a proposition.

63. ['The Temples of the Jews,' p. 176.] In this passage Mr. Fergusson suggests that a truncated column which I found in an ancient chamber under the road to Bab-as-Silsileh, 'is the identical column to which Christ was bound'—'if this is not the actual cell in which the pillar stood in which Christ was bound, it must have been in a very similar one, close at hand.'

Remarks.—It is difficult to say anything on such a subject, except to assert that there is no basis whatever for such a proposal.

THE END.

www.ingramcontent.com/pod-product-compliance
Lightning Source LLC
Chambersburg PA
CBHW020756230426
43666CB00007B/713